THE TRUTH ABOUT YOUR HEALING

(Anyone Can Be Healed of Any Disease)

Adelle Penn-Brown, D. Min

ISBN 978-1-63814-543-1 (Paperback)
ISBN 978-1-63814-544-8 (Digital)

Copyright © 2023 Adelle Penn-Brown, D. Min
All rights reserved
First Edition

All rights reserved. No part of this publication may be reproduced, distributed, or transmitted in any form or by any means, including photocopying, recording, or other electronic or mechanical methods without the prior written permission of the publisher. For permission requests, solicit the publisher via the address below.

Covenant Books
11661 Hwy 707
Murrells Inlet, SC 29576
www.covenantbooks.com

ACKNOWLEDGEMENTS

First and foremost, for every book I have written and will write in the future, it is all because of the Lord Jesus Christ's work in my life. The Holy Spirit walked me through my healing. Then He furthered me into His best, which is not getting sick but living in "immunity," which is part of the work of the cross. Every step of the way, He's been present teaching and leading me. THANK YOU, LORD.

Audain, my husband, my example, my chef, my best friend, you're the best. You're one of a kind. God designed us for each other.

My VI Christian Ministries family, you are special. As I have told you in the past and it still stands true, many pastors would love a gathering like you. You are faithful, strong in the Lord, prayer warriors, loving, and kind. We've been through much together, and we have stuck together. Persecutions and trials didn't stop us or divide us because we continued to choose God's way above everything.

Special thanks to Accra Cyntje of IMAjYNdesign. Thank you for working with me at different stages in the process. You are truly gifted, and I know there is much more planted in you just waiting for the right moment to come forth. You are truly a blessing to the body of Christ.

Special thanks to Dr. Patricia Harkins-Pierre for your edits and most importantly your support and encouragement throughout this journey.

INTRODUCTION

The work Jesus did on the cross was far greater than what most people know, understand, or preach. We all know the cross was for the sins of the world, but it is also very clear that the cross was for the healing of man's body. This is confirmed through many scriptures. In the past, there has been a shortage of healing miracles. The reason for that is because there has not been many in the body of Christ focusing on the healing miracle power of God. There are great prophecies about a great harvest. One of the avenues the Lord will and is using for the great harvest is healing miracles. We have scriptures showing after someone was healed they were saved, and many followed Him. Jesus would say, "Go and sin no more," or He would say, "Your faith has made you whole," after He healed them. That word *whole* and *saved* in Greek is *sozo*, which is the all-inclusive word used for *salvation* in the New Testament. It includes to save, to deliver or protect, to heal, to preserve, to do well and be made whole.

This book will be a nightmare for many theologians but a blessing for those who are desperate to be healed. We have confined God and His ability to our minds, but God cannot be boxed in our minds. He has His own mind, and He is revealing it to those who are hungry and interested. He is really asking us to come into His mind. As more teaching and preaching are done on healing and healing miracles, more will be seen. "Faith comes by hearing and hearing by the Word of God" (Romans 10:17).

If you are not in the position of desperation to be healed, and you believe you know everything about God and His healing miracles, then you might not understand. A word of counsel to those who, for whatever reason, are unable to see healing for physical bodies in the Word of God. Be careful you don't take hope away from those who are in a hopeless situation or those who feel hopeless and have tried everything but to no avail. Our God is the God of hope. Don't take away people's hope in the God of hope because you don't understand or it doesn't fit your theological persuasion or your experience. You're going to be held accountable for it.

Matthew 12:36 states "that every idle word that men shall speak, they shall give account thereof in the day of judgment." In this case, *idle* means "barren." If your words create barrenness, the inability to produce in someone's life, you will be held accountable for it. In other words, if someone desires to be healed, and you steal the hope or faith they had in the Word for healing through your words, you will be held accountable. You have no right to tell someone it might not be God's will for them to be healed or "Don't forget Aunt So-and-So died of the same disease you are now facing."

It doesn't matter if something seems generational. It can be changed through the most powerful words in the world, the Word of God. It's always God's will for everyone to be healed of every disease. It's in His Word. Heaven and earth will pass away, but God's word is eternal. That means it has no expiration date.

As you read this book, remember God's word is eternal, and it is filled with power because He authored it. Heaven and earth will pass away, but God's word will never pass away. Why not team up with God's word? See what it will do in your life. Going through these pages, things will be revealed to you that you have heard before but never able to grab for yourself. This book is your book for a life change. It doesn't matter if it's healing for the body, mind, or soul. You can receive it as you read, ponder, and meditate on what you are reading.

CHAPTER 1

My Beginning

One early morning—wrapped in a blanket, groggy-eyed, with sleepiness trying to take me back to bed, but resisting because I knew these moments were important—I walked to our sitting room and kneeled on the couch. In seeking the presence of the Lord, I heard.

Every day I wake early, when everything and everyone is quiet or in sleep mode, so I can have privacy with the One I have come to fall in love with and dearly love. At first, He was a stranger. He was a theological expression I learned about in Bible school. I was a believer at the age of about thirteen. I was going to heaven, but I didn't know the One who was responsible for me going there. I heard about the great men and women of faith who somehow knew Him in the way I longed but didn't know how. I heard people talk about praise and worship to enter His presence. I read the Word and prayed, but He still seemed a great mystery. I prayed in the Spirit, but He still seemed nebulous.

I was raised in the Methodist Church. I am so thankful for my parents and my upbringing. My mother played the organ, and my father was a local preacher. I attended Sunday school. My father took us to church and Sunday school. He was the Sunday school superintendent. We had to go to church. We had to be on time. We were never late. This familiarity with church life kept me from the world. I am a good example of the law leading someone to Christ.

At the age of about thirteen, I made Jesus the Lord of my life. I was forever changed. I'll never forget walking in tears down the aisle in the old Methodist Church by the Market Square to receive Jesus into my heart. I was genuinely changed on the inside. The first thing I wanted to do was pray. In our tiny two-bedroom, one-bath apartment in Estate Thomas, I waited until everyone went to bed; and then I would go into the little living room, get on my knees, and started to pray. I don't remember what I said, but every time I started to pray, with my back facing the entry door, I always felt a presence walking up the steps passing by the window, watching me, and was about to open the living room door to come to me when I'd stop and run to the bedroom. Every time that presence got close, I would stop praying and speedily go to bed. I was afraid of His presence. I never experienced anything like that. It happened every night I tried to pray. As a result, I stopped praying in the living room, because the presence continued coming every night. Instead, I started praying quietly in bed under the cover. I didn't learn until later in life it was the Holy Spirit. I was very perceptive spiritually.

Even though I stopped praying in the living room, I had a ferocious desire for God. I remember listening to R. W. Schambach on the radio every Sunday afternoon. I attended the weekly prayer meeting. Everyone in the prayer group was old enough to be my parent or grandparent. I was a child in the midst of seniors. Sometimes in the prayer meeting, we would be praying, and someone would start shaking, or they would just jump and speak a strange word. Sometimes they would speak briefly in a strange language. This was all new to me. I soon learned it was the presence of God moving in and through the person. Sometimes in the formal church service, one of the prayer group members would shout hallelujah because they felt the presence of God, and the people around would look at them in a scornful way. What many Methodists fail to realize is those were some of the things Charles and John Wesley experienced in their meetings. It was the presence of God manifesting in and through people, and that was their natural response to the supernatural.

Shortly thereafter I went on my first missionary trip with the prayer group to the beautiful island of Anguilla. There was no electricity on the island at that time. We stayed in a couple rented houses. During the day, we prayed, street-witnessed; and in the evening, we held services at the old Methodist Church. My first experience with a demon-possessed person was on that missionary trip. That missionary trip shaped the course of my life for ministry even though at the time I didn't understand fully what was happening. Many supernatural things happened on that trip. People got born again; things happened.

People say God doesn't change a personality when a person receives Christ as their Savior. I disagree. I was born to die. I was always sick. I can't remember having a healthy childhood. I was in and out of the hospital, in and out of the clinic. One time, my mother called her siblings and told them if they wanted to see me alive for the last time, to visit me at the hospital that night. I was sickly. God's mind was for me to be in this earth, living a healthy life, doing the work of the ministry. But everything contradicted that.

My parents took me through the public health system. Doctors from the United States rotated coming to the island and worked in the clinic for a duration of time in the public health system. I had already been going to the clinic for several years, taking their medication, when one day a new doctor came and asked the nurse, how long was I on a particular medication? When they told him, he was shocked and told them to immediately take me off the medication. They then immediately discharged me from the public health system. Today I understand why they moved so quickly to stop the treatment and discharge me. I was taking medication for a long time for a problem that didn't exist. That doesn't help your body; it harms your body. It weakens your body.

That along with other ailments affected me. I was tall and very thin. Children can be very mean. My classmates in elementary school used to call me "far from the kitchen," "broomstick," just to name a couple (I can laugh about that today). I became a bully because of the hurt inside and the necessity to protect myself. I hung around the wrong people at school. They protected me from the bullies. If my parents would have ever found out, I would have been in terrible trouble. I was the saint on Sunday and at home, but the bully at school. I would pick fights in school and tell the person to meet me after school to finish the fight.

After school, I disappeared. If my parents ever found out, I would not have made it to the age of thirteen to give my heart to the Lord. When that happened, I changed. My personality changed. I went from a bully picking fights and cursing to a person who hardly spoke and basically kept to myself.

I had many good experiences with the Lord, but no one could explain what was happening. That's why I stayed to myself. In addition, I didn't fit the group. A few years later, I learned it was the Holy Spirit. He had set me apart for His purpose. This might seem like I had a special calling. Yes, I did but we all have a special calling. It is special to you and you alone. It is to be fulfilled the way the Lord intended, not like how everyone else has done it. That's what makes it a special calling. It is designed only for you because it's to be fulfilled based on your uniqueness.

I believe when we are born again, not even the sky is the limit. I believe if a person continues to follow the Lord wholeheartedly, they will do great exploits for His kingdom. I believe we qualify ourselves for ministry by seeking Him and following Him. When we are born of His Spirit it's because we responded to the call. He called us out of darkness into His marvelous light, and we responded. The key is if we will do what He desires to be qualified. The Bible says, "Many are called, few are chosen."

When I made Jesus the Lord of my life, I knew I was called to the fivefold ministry. There's never been a doubt. And my heart has always been for missions. The island of Anguilla whetted my appetite. I finished high school, went to college; completed four years in three and used the remaining scholarship money to pay my Bible school tuition and expenses. There is where I learned about the Holy Spirit. The Word of God is the Truth, and miracles, signs and wonders are for the believers.

I returned home after Bible school and was given a group of hungry people to pastor. The fullness of my calling isn't pastoring. I was assigned to pastor by God because of the hungry people, and I needed to learn many things. We were good for each other. I was stretched and forced to become the word, and they grew and were stretched as a result of the ministry of the Word. Attending Bible school and living it were two different things for me. Pastoring made them one. I got married, and on our honeymoon I was in the hospital having surgery. That's how sickly I was.

Fast forward, the Holy Spirit was not where I wanted Him in my life. I was desperate in two areas. I was desperate for a healing miracle—to just have a season in my life when I felt good—no pain, no problem, and I was also desperate to know Him and have the same relationship Adam had with Him before sin. I was so desperate for that relationship with Him. From the time I got saved, I always believed it was possible for such a relationship. I also knew the only person who could make me well was Him. I started the journey to really know Him. And in prayer that morning, seeking His presence, I heard Him say to me, *If you feed on me, you will live.* I knew what I heard. That really started my desperate pursuit to know Him like Adam did.

I first needed to find what He said to me in the scriptures. I started searching the Bible, using the Strong's Concordance and I couldn't find it. One day I was reading and I found the exact words, "if you feed on me, you will live." It is John 6:57. It was the New King James Version. I usually use the NASB translation.

When I found the translation, I instantly knew what He meant and what I needed to do. In this day and age, we are all looking for instant. That was not my case in this particular instance of needing healing. It was gradual based on me following the Lord's instructions. I was already healed according to His Word, but my body needed to become the Word. I needed the revelation. It was a gradual process. Today I can look back and say this was necessary and important for me. Through the progression, I learned many, many things of my Father and experienced God in a way I never before had. It was worth it all.

Psalm 107:20 says, "He sent His Word and healed them…" Jesus is the Word made flesh (John 1:14) sent to earth for humanity. What it meant was, if I would spend my time in the Word knowing Him, I would be healed. Whatever occupies your mind controls you and it becomes a part of you. I knew I was to spend my time in the Gospels because Jesus, the Word made flesh was the *key* to my healing and the *key* in the Gospels.

Every day I read one of the Gospels. I had an order: Monday was Matthew, Tuesday was Mark, Wednesday was Luke, and Thursday was John. This was my schedule for a long season. Sometimes because Luke was longer, I would finish reading Luke on Thursday and then move to John on Friday. This was what I did to experience the fullness of John 6:57. This is what I was led to do. I wanted to receive directly from the word of God not through an anointing on a person. The wonderful experience of receiving direct from the Word emboldens you to believe because you know from experience the Word works. Desperation and hunger cause people to do things they normally would not do.

A couple things happened while in my routine for that season. One was my focus moved off the ailment; it didn't occupy my mind anymore. This is powerful. Many people are focused on the ailment and when is the pain or ailment going to disappear. You will possess your focus. Change your focus and you change the outcome. If you are sick, change the focus of sickness and put it on Jesus, and the outcome will change. The disease will leave and you wouldn't even know it. That was a major problem for me. I now understand why my assignment from Him was to read Matthew, Mark, Luke, John. I was steeped so long in sickness; that sickness was what I knew best. I lived to accommodate it. All my recollections of childhood included sickness.

Secondly, there was a power in my innermost being I didn't know I had that started to manifest. When I spoke, I was a lion. My words had substance. It was backed with power. This was my journey to health and healing this time. Before I was flailing; up one minute, down the other. Unsure, faithless; all based on following the symptoms instead of following Him. That's what many people do. If no pain, I'm healed. If there is pain, our thought pattern is either *I thought, I was healed* or *I'm not healed*. These thoughts indicate where your faith is, or what the enemy wants you to think. He wants you in the land of doubt.

THE TRUTH ABOUT YOUR HEALING

God has healed me many times and in many different ways. Sometimes, my healing came through prayer. Other times, because of it being an outright evil attack, the revealed Word; other times, Freddy Clark, a minister of God who is a seer, has been the avenue whereby I have been healed. Sometimes hands were laid on me. I have been healed by going to sleep every night with a handkerchief that David Hogan prayed over and me putting it on my body (Acts 19:11–12). Healing has come to me through warring with the Word. And as stated before I have received healing simply through the Word, me and God in fellowship and communion. I love the last method the best. That's when I started to know Him for who He really is.

Throughout the years of me needing healing and studying the Word regarding healing, God has taught me that everyone can be healed of any disease. This might sound like blasphemy to some; to others it might be considered false doctrine and to others it might be simply too hard to believe and then for others, its hope restored. He is God. His hand is not short. He wants you so much to walk in His reality for your life that He has established many avenues of healing in the body of Christ. No matter what side of the fence you are on, the truth is "Anyone can be healed of any disease."

Genesis 25:8 says, "Then Abraham breathed his last and died in a good old age, an old man and full of years." "And when Jacob had finished commanding his sons, he drew his feet up into the bed and breathed his last, and was gathered to his people" (Genesis 49:33). Isaac died the same way as Abraham and Jacob. He gave up the ghost, was gathered to his people and was old and full of days. Even though Elisha died his bones were still full of the supernatural power of God (2 Kings 13:20–21) that a man who was dead was revived.

I will prove it through the Scriptures. God wants you healed. He wants you and me walking in the fullness of what His Son did for us on the cross. It's easy to receive forgiveness of sin when committed, but difficult for healing. It shouldn't be. Sickness and sin both have the same source and the same cure; believe what Jesus did on the cross. You are never too old to be healed. You don't have to leave this earth sick. As the earth is filled with the knowledge of the glory of God, so does His healing power fill the earth. The earth is filled with the healing power of God. Healing and miracles are a sign that His kingdom is present. It's a matter of tapping into it to release it.

CHAPTER 2

Where It All Began

This goes all the way back even before man's beginning. Before there was time, God was, God is, and God will be. In God's dialogue with Job, He asked Job, where was he when He laid the foundations of the earth? Psalm 102:25 in the Passion Translation reads, "With Your hands you once formed the foundations of the earth and handcrafted the heavens above." With the creation of the foundation of the earth, time was created. We were chosen by God before the foundation of the world with purpose (Ephesians 1:4). This makes sense. God created earth for man; God made earth suitable for man whom He had chosen before the foundation of the earth. Man existed in God's heart even before He made the planet. The earth was made for man to live and rule. Imagine, you were in God's heart and mind before the earth's foundation was laid. This indicates how special we are to God. It indicates how much He loves us.

Some people believe man was made for the Sabbath. This is totally false. Jesus made it very clear; the Sabbath was made for man. The earth wasn't made for God's enemy. God cast him from heaven down to earth because He knew His creation, man, would be able to rule over him. Earth was the temporary place of judgment for God's enemy. Kicked out of heaven to temporarily live on earth and ruled by man, a lower creation, even temporarily, is judgment.

Eden was the place of delight and pleasure. They enjoyed the pleasure of the Lord's presence. Now they lost everything because they disobeyed God and were thrown out of the garden for their own protection. There were two trees in the middle of the garden of Eden. Only one they were not allowed to eat, the tree of the knowledge of good and evil. There were no restrictions set on the tree of life. They could have chosen that tree but instead, they chose the one that imparted death. In Revelation 22, in the new Jerusalem, we again see the tree of life which bares twelve fruits and leaves which are for the healing of nations. The qualification to eat from the tree of life is doing His commandments. The curiosity of the unknown is still haunting man. Like children, we are told to do or not do something and that deadly Adamic nature does the exact opposite. But there's a cure for that as well.

Adam gave his authority to the one he was to rule. In so doing, Adam died (Genesis 2:16–17). Death is first separation from God. Adam immediately died when he partook of the tree of the knowledge of good and evil. He no longer had fellowship with God. He no longer communed with God. He no longer was privy to the presence and glory of God. The result of that death which was spiritual led to physical death. The death of separation from God manifested in the natural, physical death. Physical death was the effect of spiritual death. Separation from the creator was the death that opened the door to physical death.

People wonder why God put the two trees in the garden. God didn't create evil. He created beings with the power of choice, to choose good or evil. God didn't want robots. He wanted and wants people to make choices and preferably the right choice. Adam and Eve were free to choose for themselves. They knew the consequences.

The wonderful thing about God is He tells you the consequences of your choice, then encourages you to choose the right way. He did that with Adam; He did it with the children of Israel (Deuteronomy 30:19), and He does it with us. Every day from the moment we wake until we go to bed, we are confronted with choices based on our free will. In the arena to choose, the options or choices are either good or evil. Adam was confronted to make a decision when he listened to God's enemy and he choose evil even though he knew the consequences. You'll always be confronted to choose when you listen to more than one voice. The consequences of Adam's choice made Adam the ruler to become the ruled. Some of the consequences of his choice were death instead of life, sickness instead of health, torment instead of peace. This continued from generation to generation until—

Nothing ever takes God by surprise. Adam chose. God knew what choice Adam would make and there was a plan already in place and done to fix the problem. Revelations 13:8 identifies, "the lamb slain from the foundation of the world." The whole creation was affected by Adam's decision. The results of disobedience to God's command (Genesis 3:16–17) are found in Genesis 3:12–19. A curse came on the whole earth, but along with the curse came the prophetic word of deliverance for the whole human race and creation, which was going to be birthed by Adam and Eve.

CHAPTER 3

Effects of the Curse

The effects of the curse in the first generation are first manifested in fear. That's why they sewed fig leaves together to cover their bodies. The curse manifested in the second generation through anger, murder and lying. Cain killed his brother Abel because of jealousy. God accepted his brother's offering but not his. As time progressed, the further man moved away from the presence of God, the worse things became, and God repented that He had made man. Something else that progressed with time was man's life span reversed; it became shorter and shorter. The greatest punishment for killing his brother was, he was far removed from the presence of God. The ground also no longer produced for him. In the presence of God is where His life is found; outside of God's presence is death, and Cain recognized that.

What is happening today with the invasion of sicknesses and diseases in and against the human body and the environment are all manifestations of the earth in the hands of depraved men like Cain, led by evil spirits, but that is changing. Saints, holy people of God, are arising and saying, "No more, we want it the way God intended it to be. We want God's presence covering the whole earth. We are in agreement with God and to that end we work."

Before God pronounced the curses, He went down the chain of His creation to where the disobedience began. It began when the serpent spoke to Eve. In deceiving Eve, the serpent's curse was twofold: natural and spiritual. The serpent used a serpent to entice and deceive Eve. The devil is known as the *old serpent* in the book of Revelation. We see the term *serpent* for the first time in Genesis 3:1 which makes reference to an animal because "he was more subtle (crafty) than any beast of the field which the Lord God had made."

It seems like the devil instigated the serpent (based on its nature) to raise doubt in Eve's mind about what the Lord said. In other words because of his craftiness, he was a viable animal the devil could easily enter and control. Thousands of years later the devil is doing the same thing to humanity. He raises doubts about salvation. He raises doubts about healing. He even raises doubts about the existence of God. Anything that brings pleasure to God he tries to destroy by first using doubt. That's why you have been targeted. You give God pleasure. Doubt then opens the door to unbelief. That is his modus operandi. Then you start questioning God's love because things are not going the way you expected. We live in a world that tries to dismiss the existence of God. When God is dismissed there are adverse effects. Things happen that shouldn't. Man does things that are evil (Romans 1:18–32).

When people listen to the second voice—the devil, they do things contrary to God and it affects a multitude of people. Something negative that happens in one country affects other people in different parts of the world, even more so if it's heard because hearing is the gateway to your spirit and soul.

The first pronouncement of judgment from the Lord to the serpent was it would forever crawl on its belly and eat dust all the days of its life. This has both spiritual and natural significance. Based on Genesis 3:14, the serpent is cursed above all the animals. It would crawl on its belly which leads to the idea that the serpent originally was upright. If crawling is the curse; then the serpent didn't crawl before the curse. In addition, it would eat dust. There is scientific proof that snakes occasionally lick the ground or pick up dust particles to smell its surroundings. Then there is the spiritual component which is for the devil. There would be and, is hostility between the devil and the woman, and between the serpent's seed and the woman's seed.

What a contradiction. The seed normally comes from the man, but in this prophetic word, the seed is supernatural. This is the virgin birth which is the Messiah prophesied. The seed of the woman, Jesus, would bruise the head of the serpent. In the process, the seed of the serpent would bruise (overwhelm, break, snap) his heel. We see Jesus endured the cross, the shame, and overcame the persecutions. He was mocked, beaten, crucified with purpose. What appeared to be Jesus's demise (the bruising) by the enemy, was actually the beginning of victory for all humanity. Jesus stripped the enemy of his power. He defeated satan. He took the keys of death and Hades, and rose from the dead declaring, "All authority and power is given unto Me." This is the woman's seed bruising the head of satan, the serpent. The blow Jesus gave satan ultimately destroyed him. The head of any business, organization, family, country is the seat of authority and power. Jesus took all authority and power satan had, leaving him with none. That is the bruising of his (satan's) head. He is powerless.

When Jesus rose from the dead and boldly declared all authority was given to Him in heaven and earth, notice Jesus never released it totally to man the way Adam had it. He tells us to *go* and He is with us always. He commissions us. What He did was those who believed in Him and what He did, would access His power. Today, many people are trying to live life without God. The quality of life we desire only comes through walking with Him the same way Adam did. Many people are living unfulfilled lives because they are living without Him.

That's why when you are born again, the scriptures refer to us being *in Him*. When we are *in Him* that means His authority flows through to us. It is not released to everyone. It's to those who love Him so much that they would obey Him. What happened with Adam will never happen again to the whole human race because He—Jesus, conquered God's enemy, and now has an earthly and heavenly title, and His heavenly glory is restored.

Every day, we all have two trees from which we choose. We can choose the tree of life or the tree of the knowledge of good and evil.

Everything from the tree of life gives life. The tree of life has twelve fruits, and the leaves are for the healing of the nations. If healing and divine health are your desire, then every day, eat from the tree of life. Sickness was never a part of God's equation for man. It was always life, and it will always be life.

CHAPTER 4

The Two Voices

When God created man, He made him in His image. He was given authority to rule and reign in the earth. He was given dominion over everything including everything that moved on the earth. He was placed in Eden to rule. In the garden were also two trees. Every tree of the garden was food for man with the exception of one. He was told in the day he ate from that specific tree he would die.

Entering the garden was a serpent that challenged the most vulnerable one, Eve. According to Genesis 2:16–17, God gave the command to Adam. Eve was created after God spoke to Adam about the tree in the middle of the garden. Adam told Eve what God said. We know this because she rehearses it to the serpent when he approaches her. It is also obvious that the serpent was present when God instructed Adam or Adam instructed Eve. We know this because the serpent is the one who starts the conversation with Eve in a question format, "Has God really said you shouldn't eat of every tree of the garden?"

He flips the question. Eve adds to what she was told. The serpent tells Eve that God knows if she eats of it her eyes will be opened and she'll become like God. Genesis 3:22, God says that the man has become like Us, to know good and evil.

God's plan was Adam and Eve ruling and having dominion in purity. Once you are filled and overflowing; if you listen, the second voice will always throw you into chaos. There is no purity in the second voice. The second thought always brings doubt. The second voice is to question and overthrow the first—truth. Remember the devil is not creative. He doesn't know what God wants to say to you in advance. He has to hear it first, then he puts a twist on it to create doubt. His question to create doubt is, "Was that God or me?" Because he operates out of and in darkness, he hears what's in the light and twists it to create doubt and unbelief. The devil doesn't know everything. He is a created being. If he knew what God's plan was for man and him, he would never have crucified the Lord of glory (1 Corinthians 2:8).

To have dominion and rule is easier done when there's not a dichotomy in thinking or voices. Right now there is a dichotomy of your thoughts about being healed and delivered. I know this because if there wasn't, you would be walking in your miracle. This might seem hard to believe, but the minute you start listening to only one voice, the right voice, your world is going to change. I listened to the two voices for a long time. The one voice which was based on the Word of God became stronger than the one which was speaking on behalf of the symptoms. The healing power of God flows easily when there is a vessel not hearing two voices. You see scriptures referring to your healing, but your mind wouldn't let you hold fast to that thought.

You are thinking, *Yes, the Word says I was healed*; but your mind, because of symptoms and what the reports have been saying to you, hinders your ability to believe. Adam and Eve were fine until they started listening to satan's voice.

Eve's position was to rule over the serpent, not have conversation with him. Who you have conversations with will always influence your life's choices, especially after you have clearly heard the Lord's voice. Sometimes those closest to you will bring the second voice which creates doubt and unbelief to the first voice, the truth. There are only two voices in the world, good and evil. Every human being speaks from one of those two places. They could be speaking on behalf of the first voice or the second voice, the good voice or the evil voice.

This is what happened to Eve. The Bible says, "Adam was not deceived, but Eve was." The definition in the Strong's Concordance for *deceive* is to cheat (i.e., delude). *Delude* means (1) to make someone believe something that is not true, (2) to fool yourself into believing something is true because you want it to be true, when it is actually not true (https://dictionary.cambridge.org). This definition is very interesting. Eve was deceived. She believed something that was not true. She responded to the serpent that the tree in the midst of the garden she was not to eat. There were two trees in the midst of the garden, the tree of life and the tree of the knowledge of good and evil. Only one tree in the midst of the garden they were forbidden to eat.

Eve heard two voices: "Don't eat from that particular tree, or else you will die" was the first voice; the second voice came after, which is why it's second, and said, "You certainly will not die." Doubt enters. Then the serpent continues. He hooks her by telling her God knows the day she eats it, she will become like Him, knowing good and evil. The doubt creates mistrust of God's Word, like He is intentionally withholding information. Then she looked at the tree again, and based on the knowledge the serpent gave her and the beauty of the fruit, she convinced herself to eat it. All that God had told her was negated with one question.

The type of relationship they had with God forever changed because she entertained a question from the serpent which led to their decision which caused death. Always follow the first voice. "A double minded man is unstable in all his ways." *Double-minded* means "twice." That means you are hearing something similar but not the same. And the Bible continues and says, "For let not that man suppose that he will receive anything from the Lord."

Adam's situation was different from Eve's. God spoke directly to him. He knew the consequences of eating from that tree. He was right there listening to his wife speak to the serpent (Genesis 3:6). He knew the nature of the serpent. He was the one that named him. Adam knew the serpent was an enchanter and cunning and he still allowed him to continue. Adam even allowed himself to get hooked into what he was saying. When Eve spoke to him to eat the fruit, he was actually hearing Eve's voice but listening to the serpent speaking through her. Adam knew better; that's why the Bible says, "He wasn't deceived."

Eve's disobedience led to tremendous pain in childbirth and problems during pregnancy for women. She would have a longing, a strong desire for her husband, and he would rule over her. In other words, she would be subject to him. Before they were ruling together, now Adam rules over her. The New Living Translation states, "And you will desire to control your husband, but he will rule over you."

Today many men have relinquished their authority in the home. That's many times why men perceive their wives as nags. When authority is used in the environment it was created, it ends nagging and the perception of nagging. It was created to work in the environment of love manifested by patience, peace, gentleness, goodness, faith, meekness, temperance and most of all healthy communication and responsibility.

Because Adam listened to his wife, creation turned against him. Nothing produced for him the way it was in the beginning. His work would be tremendously difficult because creation is no longer listening to him. His relationship with God is broken and so is his relationship with creation. The ground was cursed because of his action. Before the ground was blessed, now there were weeds and thorns. He now has to sweat and work all day to produce a harvest.

Another result of his disobedience was his body returns to the dust from which it came. It was never God's intent for man to die physically, but disobedience brought death. The ground is cursed and everything that came from it (Genesis 3:17). Therefore, man's body is also under the same sentence. That is why it returns to the ground. That is why you are sick, diseased in your body or simply getting older. But there is *great news* ahead. Keep reading.

CHAPTER 5

God Found a Friend in the Earth

As man continued to be fruitful and multiply, and wickedness increased, God had already worked His plan to bruise the head of the serpent. And satan didn't see it coming. Nothing takes God by surprise. He knows everything before it happens. From the foundation of the world, everything that needed to be done to redeem man was done. It was a matter of man walking through His plan. For His plan to manifest, He sought a man who would believe Him so faith in Him would be reestablished in the earth. As a result of Adam's disobedience, man's heart continually got darker and more perverted. Man stopped calling on the Lord. He actually became the enemy of God. His nature was the exact opposite of his creator. As Jeremiah 17:9 states, "The heart is deceitful above all things and desperately wicked."

Man's heart was desperately wicked. It was so wicked that he couldn't stand before God. He was in a hole full of death and darkness and there was no way out. He began to think he was God. Then he started worshipping the creatures instead of the creator. This was all the serpent's plan; to remove man totally from the presence of God and to remove man's memory of and from the presence of the Lord. His plan was to destroy the apple of God's eye. And it was working very well; or so it seemed.

When Adam relinquished his authority to the serpent, God no longer had the ability to rule the earth through Adam as was intended. God had given Adam authority to rule on earth like He does in heaven. As God reigned in heaven, so was Adam to reign on the earth. Because Adam had the nature of God, he was capable of ruling like God did in heaven but on earth.

In essence God would rule through Adam. Psalm 115:16 states, "The heaven, even the heavens, are the Lord's: but the earth hath He given to the children of men." There was a problem. God no longer had free reign and access on earth because Adam, the person through whom it was to be done, was now against God based on his choice. In essence God was locked out of the earth He created because of Adam's disobedience. The only way back into the earth was through a man like God initially planned with Adam. Adam was now ruling the earth, but under the control of the serpent for the serpent.

A well-known historic revivalist, one of the Wesley brothers, made the statement (paraphrased), "It seems God's hands are tied in the earth unless someone prays." In looking at the history of man that seems to be accurate. Ezekiel 22:30–31 reveals God's heart. He says, "I sought for a man among them that should make up the hedge and stand in the gap before me for the land that I should not destroy it: but I found none. Therefore have I poured out mine indignation upon them; I have consumed them with the fire of my wrath: their own way have I recompensed upon their heads, saith the Lord God."

It is clear God did not want His wrath released but He had no choice because no one would pray. He is the God of justice. Justice from God is love. The result was His just judgment. The priests had violated the law, polluted God's holy things and profaned the Sabbaths among other things. The princes killed and destroyed the people for dishonest gain. The prophets were saying things in the name of the Lord that He did not say. The people in the land were oppressed, robbed, vexed, and needy. The stranger was also oppressed. God looked for one person to stand between judgment and the people, and He found none. Not one righteous person was found to pray to stay the impending doom. Imagine the power of a righteous person that prays. Unfortunately in Ezekiel, not one person was found to stay the hand of righteous judgment. Prayer is God's invitation to man to invite Him into our worlds.

God is still looking for those who would stand-in the gap for the earth, for the nations of the world and for the peoples and tribes. God looked and He found Seth, Adam's last son.

"And to Seth, to him also there was born a son and he called his name Enos; then began men to call upon the name of the Lord" (Genesis 4:26). So up until that time from Adam to Seth, man stopped calling on the name of the Lord. As the generations passed up until Noah, sin increased. "And God saw that the wickedness of man was great in the earth and every imagination of the thoughts of his heart only evil continually. And it repented the Lord that He had made man on the earth and it grieved Him at His heart." In God looking for a man at this time He found Noah, who was seven to eight generations from Seth. Noah was just and walked with the Lord. God was going to extinguish the darkness in the earth with the exception of Noah and his family.

Noah built an ark in accordance to God's will and plan, loaded food and several of each type of animal in the ark and God closed the ark. It rained forty days and forty nights, and the waters started to lower after one hundred fifty days. God kept Noah and his descendants alive by locking them in the ark while the earth was flooded by water. Everything and everyone in the ark survived the flood. When they came out of the ark, Noah burnt offerings to the Lord, got drunk from the vineyard he had grown; and his son, Ham was disrespectful to his father. He saw his father was naked and told his brothers. Noah cursed Ham's son, Canaan. Canaan and his descendants became a servant to all his brothers and their descendants.

Even though man had a new beginning with Noah, sin still haunted man because it was in his blood. It shows up in Noah's son, Ham sinning against his father. There's no way to remove sin from man except through the blood of Jesus. Sin is in man's blood. To change the blood you need a transfusion. The whole human race was dead to God, sinful in nature. But there was a lineage that started seeking God and it was through Shem, Noah's son.

God sought a man and found a man from the descendants of Shem, Noah's son. God followed the family lineage of Shem to find a man who would trust Him wholeheartedly. While the serpent was working his plan, God had already implemented His plan with a man called Abram. Faith in God was reintroduced into the earth through Abraham who believed God. He became God's friend and the lineage from which the Messiah came.

Through Abraham, God made a way to turn things around. God did something very amazing with Abraham that opened the door to Him being able to move in the earth again.

He did something that no one saw coming, not even the serpent, satan. It would forever start the change of the direction of the world. Before, the serpent had all rule, reign, and authority but it started to end when God did this one thing. No one expected God to do this.

CHAPTER 6

Covenant

The self-existent God cut a covenant with a human called Abram. God came to Abram with His plan, His desire. Abram agreed. Covenants are very powerful especially when God is involved. It gives access to places that were inaccessible. It gives access to the impossible. It gives protection. God's covenants reveal His heart, His will and His love. In God making a covenant with Abram, He bound Himself to him and his progeny for better or worse forever. God's covenant with Abram gave Abram what he could never access and that was a son. He was too old and his wife was old and was also very barren before she was old. This is hopeless beyond hope. But because Abraham believed God, he was able to have an heir which was very important to Abram. Having a son was very important to him. It was important culturally. It was also very important to God because Abram's faith in God put him in right standing with God. And that relationship produced the lineage in which God used to send His son. God found someone He could trust with the fate of humanity.

The history of Abraham before God introduced Himself to him was Abram's father, Terah, took Abram; Lot, his grandson, whose father died in Ur; and his daughter in law, Sarai to Haran.

The plan was to go to Canaan but they instead settled in Haran. Terah, Abram's father died in Haran, and they stayed there. They settled. They no longer pursued Canaan. Don't settle. Don't be half-hearted about your desire. Go after it; pursue it. Sacrifice for it. Your sacrifice not only blesses you and puts you into a new and better season but also those who come behind you. Settling with sickness is still the curse operating in your life. Whatever controls you, you are a slave to it. Break all agreements and chains with the curse. The *way* has been made.

The Holy Spirit is with you to bring it to pass. With Him you can do anything and everything. This applies to every area of your life.

In Haran, the Lord told Abram to leave his country, Haran, where he had settled his relatives and his father's house to go to a land which He, the Lord, would show him. The land where the Lord was going to take Abram was to Canaan which is where they originally set forth to go. Canaan was over five hundred miles from Haran. It was a long journey from Ur to Haran and then to Canaan. On the heels of telling him to leave everything behind, He also told him what He would do for him in his obedience. He was going to make him a great nation. Bless him, make his name great; make him a blessing. Bless those who bless him and curse those who curse him; and in him, all the families of the earth would be blessed.

The Lord started the process of cutting a covenant with Abram by first testing his obedience. Covenants are not arbitrarily cut with anyone. It's done with purpose and intentionality. It has to be someone in which there is something in common. Remember, God introduced Himself to Abram while his family worshiped other gods. Marriage is a covenant relationship. Even in marriage your partner should be someone who shares certain things in common with you. The most important thing you and your partner should have in common is relationship with God through the Lord Jesus Christ. The more you have in common spiritually with your spouse, the easier and greater things will be accomplished between the two of you. Once Christ and the ways of Christ are central, then the two can overcome anything. Christ must be central.

There had to be a common thread that would allow God to work with Abraham. That thread was faith which led to obedience. That was very significant. Faith in God is the foremost thing God requires of everyone. Faith in God will bring everything into order.

God starts His relationship with Abram by telling him to leave his country, family, and his father's house. Meaning, leave everything that's familiar, and He would take him to a different land. He also told him He would make him a great nation. He would bless him, make his name great. Curse those who cursed him, and all the families of the earth would be blessed. He left everything behind except Lot, his nephew, who had lost his father at a young age. He was seventy-five years old when he started his journey with the Lord. You are never too old to start your journey with the Lord. The key is to start.

The instructions God gave Abram to leave everything behind and follow Him are the same instructions He gives us today. We leave everything behind in the new birth, and by His Spirit we are able to follow Him like Abram followed Him. The concept of your journey with God implies change along the way to fully become what's necessary to inherit what God has prepared for you. Don't underestimate the power in the new birth and being led by the Holy Spirit. You become a totally different person. The shell which is the outside might continue to look the same, but the inside is totally different. Don't underestimate the tests along the way. With every test there is a reward. God tested Abram along the way.

Abram responded totally to God's directive with one exception; he took Lot, his nephew with him. As Abram journeyed, he entered Canaan, and the Lord appeared to him and told him He would give his descendants the land of Canaan. Abram built an altar to the Lord at the place the Lord gave him that word. After Lot separated from him, he built another altar to the Lord. The altar was built after the Lord told him to walk through the land He was going to give him and his seed. In addition, at that time He told Abram his seed would be like the dust of the earth and if it could be numbered that's how many there would be.

The Lord is hilarious. He makes me laugh. He always tells us things that are impossible. The wonderful thing is those impossibilities He shows and tells us, is His reality for us. And all He requires of us is to believe and walk the journey with Him. He never asks us to do the impossible unless we are with Him. He says, "By His Son's stripes you were healed." That's His reality. That's heaven's reality.

That's kingdom's reality. He never asks us to do our earthly reality. He only asks us to believe and do His reality. The most amazing thing is when you believe; it becomes your reality. When we all believe, it becomes our reality. Know that God's reality for you is going to be tested on its way to earth, but remember you are from heaven. So you can believe by agreeing with heaven's reality and it will be. It will become earth's reality.

Abraham's faith in God's reality was tested when God told him to offer up his son, Isaac, for a burnt offering. Abraham did what the Lord told him. His son Isaac recognized the altar was built. The fire and the wood were present, but there was no offering. Isaac made the comment and his father told him, the Lord would provide a lamb for the burnt offering. God promised Abraham a son. He knew enough of God's nature to know the end would not be Isaac's death. He knew God keeps His promises. He knew God had the ability to raise Isaac from the dead if necessary. If He gave him a son which was impossible, certainly He can raise him from the dead. God's promise to Abraham was he would have seed, and if the dust of the earth could be counted, that's how many he would have.

God's promise when believed activates the power that's been lying dormant in the promise so it does happen. When we believe the promise, it is transferred from heaven to earth. Our faith in God's promise is what moves God's reality from heaven to us. It becomes our reality. It happens.

Just think how amazing it is that in the new birth we are created to think like God. We can believe like God. We can transport what's in heaven to earth through God's faith. In essence, what God wants us to realize is nothing, absolutely nothing is impossible and faith in Him is not difficult.

Every promise of God is supernatural because it comes from God. However, the power in the promise lies dormant until it's placed in the right environment. The power in the promise comes alive because the promise is placed in the right soil and environment. Every word of God, when spoken and believed, has the power in itself to create. The difference is the person. It's like a seed planted in soil. In the seed is a potential plant, flower or fruit. Whether it happens or not depends on the environment where it is placed. A major key in the development of the plant, flower or fruit from the seed is the soil which is typified to be the heart of man. This is the parable of the sower.

If the environment is poor, the seed remains infertile. The environment makes the seed fertile. Every promise of God apart from a person is not productive. The book we call the Bible doesn't do anything for us unless it is placed in the heart of man. It's a book until the words on the pages are placed in the heart of man. The promises were created for people. They work in and through people. God's promises were created to become fertile in the heart of man which is the soil, grow and produce a harvest. It's like the word of God in the book called the Bible. Unless someone picks up the Bible, reads it and believes it, nothing happens. It remains a good book. It remains a book filled with seed promises waiting to be placed in the soil and watered and gardened to bring forth a harvest.

God's word is sure. How many times have we aborted a seed because we gave up or we didn't persevere? This is the season to not give up. This is the season to persevere. This is harvest time. I have a mango tree. It was planted in the ground. On the surface it seemed like the tree was doing absolutely nothing. I couldn't see any growth for a long time. One day while outside, I looked at the tree and it was growing. Then a year later, I saw a little funny round shaped thing on a branch. When I looked, it was a tiny mango. Even though it seemed to me like it wasn't growing; it was.

What I didn't see was what was happening with the roots. The roots were going deep in the soil so the wind wouldn't blow it over. We had two hurricanes about a month apart and the tree remained. The heavy wind and rain from the hurricanes; nor the hot sun could kill the tree. It's still around and producing sweet mangoes. Don't give up. I have to confess that I very rarely watered the tree and I did not fertilize it. It was the rains from heaven that caused it to produce mangos. If I watered it consistently, it would have grown faster. The rate of growth was dependent on me. My husband was constantly saying to me, "How do you expect mangoes if you are not watering the tree?"

He was right. It's the same with the word of God. You plant the word, water it regularly and you'll start to see the little fruit of healing. Many people get excited at that juncture and stop. You have to keep doing it until you have mangos ready to be plucked from the tree.

What soil are you? If you don't like the type of soil you are, you can change it. If you are not producing plants, flowers or fruits, check the soil; check your heart. You can make yourself good soil. You can turn your heart into good soil. You do this first by weeding; removing the unforgiveness, bitterness, anger, malice, offenses, and fear from your heart. Do this through true repentance. Psalm 51 is a good example of a repentant heart. This is written by David after Nathan disclosed his sin to him with Bathsheba and Uriah, her husband.

Next, continue planting and watering seeds of healing. Find scriptures for your healing and meditate on them day and night. "My son, give attention to my words; incline your ear to my sayings. Do not let them depart from your eyes; keep them in the midst of your heart; for they are life to those who find them and health to all their flesh (Proverbs 4:20–22). You can use my other book *63 Days ± to Your Healing* to assist with scriptures and meditation.

In the NLT, verses 23–27 of Proverbs 4 state, "Guard your heart above all else for it determines the course of your life. Avoid all perverse talk; stay away from corrupt speech. Look straight ahead, and fix your eyes on what lies before you. Mark out a straight path for your feet; stay on the safe path. Don't get sidetracked; keep your feet from following evil." You follow evil when you remove yourself from the scriptures you are using to fight the battle. To do so will destroy the seeds growing in your life.

The Word must become your priority in everything and every area of your life. Take care of the seed. Water it. Persevere with it. Be patient with it. Water the seed with a Holy Spirit relationship with the Lord and Holy Spirit praying. Protect your relationship with the Lord and the Word. They are first in your life.

Another example is a woman conceives a child based on a seed planted in her. As she continues to eat the healthy right foods, the baby in her grows healthy. When it reaches nine months, it is ready to come forth. So it is with the Word of God planted in your heart. You eat, which is not a onetime event but continually eat as written in John 6:57. You eat according to need. The need is what you desire. You want a healthy baby, you eat healthy foods such as vegetables and of course, you take your vitamins which gives your body and the baby a healthy boost. You don't eat once a day or once a week when you are pregnant. You eat several times a day. Do the same with healing scriptures. As you eat the healthy food which is the Word of God, the seed grows and grows and the time comes when the seed is actually healing manifested.

Every encounter Abraham had with God, which is synonymous to our fellowship with the Lord, built his faith to trust God that when time came for Abraham to be tested by offering up Isaac, he didn't hesitate. He knew God. He believed the prior words God had spoken to him through his encounters with Him. Furthermore, he had proof that God was true to His word because Sarah had given birth to God's promise to him which was Isaac. Abraham obeyed the Lord and when he was about to follow through with the knife to kill Isaac, the angel of the Lord stopped him. God now knew that Abraham feared Him, revered Him. Abraham withheld nothing of magnitude from God. That was when God swore by Himself. There was no one greater to swear by. God is above everything. Everything is upheld by Him. Everything has its existence from Him. Abraham was our example. Every promise God made to us was made under an oath. And there is no one greater than God, Himself. The promise will come to pass because God swore by Himself and He cannot lie. Every promise God made to us, He swore by Himself that it will be fulfilled. The fulfillment was manifested in the cross and Jesus's resurrection.

What we have left to do is simply believe, which leads to definitive action.

What is the covenant God made with Abraham? The Abrahamic covenant is one of a series of covenants God made with the express purpose of taking man back to the original reason he was created. As stated in my book, *Immunity*, every covenant has three major parts: the words of the covenant, the blood of the covenant, and the seal of the covenant. The words of the Abrahamic covenant consists of the promises God made to Abraham. God made four promises to Abraham. God told him in Genesis 12:2–3, He would make him a great nation and bless him. He would make his name great, and he would be a blessing. Those who blessed Abraham would be blessed and who cursed him would be cursed, and in him all the families of the earth would be blessed.

Everything God did for and through Abraham comes out of the promises. For example, Abraham would become a great nation. Underlying in that statement is Abraham will have a seed. To be a nation requires an offspring. Abraham didn't know how God was going to do it because at that time, all he had was Eliezer of Damascus who was born in his house. But God, the creator of heaven and earth had a plan even before Abraham was born.

Every time God appeared to Abraham, He, God gave him a word to help him know God more so he would continue to believe and grow in faith toward the Lord. At the end of every encounter Abraham built an altar. An altar in Hebrew is a place of slaughter and sacrifice. It's a place of thanksgiving, sacrifice, commemoration.

No longer do we build altars with wood, stone and animals. Our hearts are now the altars prepared and designed only for the Lord. In the past, altars were external, physical places to worship, remember, and totally surrender to the Lord. But because of the blood of Jesus, they are now internal, which are our hearts. From our hearts we worship the Lord; we remember the Lord, and from our hearts we totally commit and recommit everything to the Lord. His life flows from our hearts. A true believer can only worship the Lord from their heart because the Lord dwells in the heart of the believer. Our hearts are eternal altars of the Lord fully connected to Him; one with Him (1 Corinthians 6:17).

CHAPTER 7

Abraham's Faith in God

As Abram obeyed God and proved himself faithful to trust the Lord, the Lord appeared to him in a vision and told him *not to fear, He was his shield, and his reward would be very great.* Abraham's response from the New Living Translation in Genesis 15:2 says, "O Sovereign Lord, what good are all your blessings when I don't even have a son? Since you've given me no children, Eliezer of Damascus, a servant in my household, will inherit all my wealth. You have given me no descendants of my own, so one of my servants will be my heir."

God's response to Abram from the Message Translation was, "Don't worry, he won't be your heir; a son from your body will be your heir." After the Lord spoke that to him, He took him outside to count the stars if he was able, because the stars were symbolic of his descendants. This was God building Abram's faith to believe. God used the stars, the dust, the name change for Abram. Abraham believed God and it was counted to him for righteousness.

For us today He uses the same method. He's given us multiple promises, like He did Abraham. Then He tells us if we would believe, all things are possible. In other words, the sky is not the limit. You set the limit. Not even God sets the limit because He has no limit. Our promises are His word. That's what builds our faith.

God tells us our potential based on His plan. When He initially tells us, it's a shocker because it's bigger than us. It's bigger than we ever thought. But in Him telling us our potential, our faith comes alive. Zeal is awakened. Joy is stirred. And hope is realized. Then your faith is tested so you can move towards fulfilling your potential. It happened with Jesus. God told Jesus His potential. "You are my son and in you I am well pleased." In Him telling Jesus He was His son, He was telling Him His potential. "You are the son of God." "You have unlimited power at your disposal." "You will change the course of humanity." Then Jesus was sent into the wilderness to be tested by the devil.

The revelation that He was the son of God and God was well pleased with Him gave Jesus the ability to stand against the enemy and overcome through the word. It's the same with you and me. The revelations we receive that we are His children, and He is pleased with us are more than enough to overcome the enemy like Jesus did. Romans 8:14 says (NKJV), "For as many as are led by the Spirit of God, these are the sons of God."

Notice God announced Jesus is His Son after the Holy Spirit descended upon Him in the form of a dove. In addition, because Jesus left His glory behind, when He descended to earth in the form of man (Philippians 2:5–8), He couldn't perform any miracles or healings as God the Son. He had to be led by the Spirit. They had to be done as a man filled with the Holy Spirit. This sets forth the example of who we would be in the new birth and the baptism in the Holy Spirit and how we would operate in the earth, which is like Jesus, the Son of God, who made us sons of God. Romans 8:29 states that Jesus is the firstborn among many brethren. Every born-again believer constitutes the "many brethren." We are like our "big brother."

The enemy always shows up to test the Word of the Lord for your life and in your life and God allows him. God allows him because you are well able and equipped with God's word and aid of the Holy Spirit to overcome him. Additionally, the strength of Christ's life in us is confirmed. The Word of the Lord is your seed potential. In that seed is all the power of God (dunamis) needed to overcome every situation and circumstance in life at your present point. To test you is to test your faith in God's word. That's why Jesus kept responding to the enemy's test with the Word of God, "It is written." The test is—do you believe God? Whose report (word) will you believe?

The power in the Word of God is what holds you in the tough times, which everyone experiences because we live in a fallen world. That word God gives you, whether it is spoken or the written Word of God, is the anchor that will hold you in the position of faith if you allow it. Sometimes there is the element of disobedience in man, when he's not to move, that's when he wants to move; and when he is to move, that's when he doesn't want to move. That place is what we call the *comfort zone* or *I can do it Lord; I don't need you for this*.

The *comfort zone* is the place where we attempt to settle or do it ourselves, failing to realize that is the place of temptation. Jesus could have settled for an earthly kingdom but that was not God's Word to Him. God's plan was much bigger than an earthly kingdom. It's the same with you. God's plan for you is much bigger than an earthly kingdom. His plan is greater and beyond. The Word He gave you is meant to war with when you are in that place of comfort or trying to do it on your own. That Word He gave you will keep you moving with Him until you reach the destination which is fulfilling your purpose. This is the place where you will experience the greatest fulfillment in life. So take the Word of healing; use it to war; don't settle for man's best. Use the Word to push you past your comfort zone and man's best. God's best is greater and it is attainable. It's yours.

The enemy's plan is to separate you from your faith in God's word. He doesn't want you to believe you are a child of God. He doesn't want you to believe you were healed. He doesn't want you to believe all things are possible. He doesn't want you to think that to believe is as easy as breathing; that it's natural. When you believe those things, you become a threat to him. When Jesus said to the demon possessed boy's father in Mark 9 regarding his son, that if he could believe all things are possible to him who believes, the father didn't have the Spirit of faith dwelling within him. He wasn't born again. He knew only the law. He knew nothing about the grace of God. We, who are born again, have the Spirit of God dwelling within us. So believing is easy.

Jesus was an enigma for the spiritual leaders of His day. Even though the Torah spoke about Him, they didn't recognize Him. When Jesus arrived on the scene, it was obvious that they had strayed from the way it was intended. There was a problem with the governance of the religious leadership and system. Jesus dealt with the problems of His day and gave His life for the problems of every day—the past, the present, and the future. The problem of every day is man's disconnect with His creator and Father. Through Jesus, that connection is restored, and it produces greater blessings in life (i.e., health, healing, peace in the middle of the storm, joy). God has faith in you. Why not reciprocate and have faith in God? You are His child. You have overcome and do overcome daily.

I read the story of Smith Wigglesworth when he and his wife pledged to each other and God that they would no longer have doctors, medicine, or drugs of any kind in their house. They were zealous for the Lord and passionate to see people healed and delivered, and they couldn't do it half-heartedly. It is so true; it is easy to make vows when everything is fine, but what counts is being faithful when the test comes. They were shortly tested after that. And they overcame.

CHAPTER 8

Jesus, the High Priest

At the last Passover, when Jesus celebrated with His disciples, He told Peter in Luke 22:31 that satan demanded to sift (to put a loose or fine substance through a sieve to remove lumps) him like wheat. Jesus didn't tell Peter the answer given to satan was *no* and he wasn't allowed; instead, Jesus told Peter, He prayed for him so his faith would not fail. Peter had to go through. In Him going through, he became a bold witness of Jesus Christ after Jesus rose from the grave. He was also the author of two books of the Bible. Under Peter's preaching over three thousand people were saved in one meeting. Jesus was the intercessor on earth for His disciples.

Today, He is our high priest in heaven who makes intercession for us. The same thing He did for Peter, He has done for us and is doing for us. Jesus's response shows what satan's intent was and is. But it also shows the power of Jesus's intercession. Satan's intent was for Peter's faith to fail. In other words, his faith would cease existing in Jesus. But Jesus prayed. Notice that even though Peter denied the Lord, he came back to the Lord. Jesus has faith in His prayers. He told Peter, "When once you have turned again, strengthen your brothers." Those were Jesus's instructions to Peter.

There was no question in Jesus's mind if Peter would return to Him. He had no doubt that Peter would return to Him. Jesus who is our great high priest makes intercession for us. Hebrews 7:25 (KJV), "Wherefore He is able also to save them to the uttermost that come unto God by Him, seeing He ever liveth to make intercession for them."

Jesus has saved us entirely. In other words, there is no situation that you do not have the victory over. Jesus has already prayed for you that your faith wouldn't fail. Rise up, believe what He says, and see the miracle working power of God released in that situation that you have already overcome. He is able to heal you totally when you go to God through Him because He's alive and making intercession for you.

See the beauty and power of this. Jesus, the Son of God, with a glorified body who is our high priest sitting on the right hand of the throne of Majesty in heaven makes intercession for us. And on earth we have the Holy Spirit who makes intercession for us and through us with groanings that are unspeakable. Because Jesus lives forever, His priesthood doesn't change and He is able to deliver, protect, heal, preserve, make whole, save continually and completely because He's making intercession for us (Hebrews 7:24–25). The Holy Spirit on earth living in the believer, prays through the believer because of the weakness of not knowing what he should specifically pray and how. The only person who knows how to pray perfectly regarding each of us individually is the Holy Spirit.

When we look at a situation we usually see it from our perspective. Even when we engage heaven for its perspective, it is still filtered through our minds unless we receive revelation which bypasses our thoughts. That's when we have the mind of the Spirit. Once it goes through a human channel meaning the mind or thoughts, it is many times tainted or filtered. But Jesus isn't concerned about that. He knows exactly what to say to us, how to say it and when to say it to us.

Jesus our High Priest (Romans 8:34) and the Holy Spirit our comforter (John 14:16) is heaven and earth working together and in harmony. This is when heaven and earth unite. The result of heaven and earth working together is all things working together for good to those who love God and are called according to His purpose. God has you covered. Don't be afraid. He wouldn't let you fall.

Heaven and earth are interceding for you according to God's purpose. You can't fail. It's not in your DNA to fail. Agree with everything God says about you no matter what it looks like. Even if you don't feel like it, push yourself a little harder and say what God says about you. If you believe you have pushed and you're exhausted or tired, then cry out to the Lord. Cry out, "Lord help me. I need Your help." It might not seem theologically correct, but that's exactly what blind Bartimaeus and the Syrophoenician woman did. God's word never fails. God's word is filled with power when we agree with it and declare it. Say it: "Heaven and earth are going to go away—it's going to perish, but God's word remains forever and ever. Amen."

Peter's faith was tested and shaken. He had lied about his relationship with Jesus. He denied he knew his master and Lord three times. He denied to the people around that he knew the one who took care of him, taught him, healed his mother-in-law. Peter was disappointed in himself. He probably was also ashamed and probably disgusted with himself. Disappointment happens because of an unexpected outcome. Peter did not expect to deny Jesus even though Jesus told him what was going to happen. Peter couldn't believe it until it happened. It happened exactly as Jesus said. Peter denied Jesus three times. When it happened, Jesus looked at Peter, and Peter remembered what Jesus said. Jesus lives out of time, but today in our time, Jesus has already prayed for you to come through in victory whatever you are facing. If it's sickness, Jesus has prayed for you to catch the revelation that you were already healed; therefore, you are healed. Jesus remembers what He did on the cross and what it meant for you. Walk in it. Speak it. Think it. Read it. Dream it. Do it.

This is where faith in our high priest prayers become powerful. The role of the high priest is to offer sacrifice for sin. The priest is the person who stands between God and man. The priest offered sacrifices for sin. But Jesus offered Himself as the sacrifice for our sins which was once and forever. He took His blood and presented it into the holy of holies in heaven not to cover over our sins like the earthly high priests did, but to totally remove our sins. The price was paid with His blood. Jesus was the high priest and the sacrifice. Now the price has been paid. No more sacrificing is necessary. His blood did a perfect work in the heavens and earth for heaven and earth.

Hebrews 4 tells us since Jesus functions from heaven as our high priest, we should hold on to our confession. If your confession is you were healed, stick to it. If it is you are prosperous, stick to it. If your confession is "I am strong," stick to it. Whatever promise you need and have found in the word of God, stick to it. He's cleared the path in heaven for it to come to earth. He's removed every obstacle that would stop you from going to the throne of grace, to receive it and bring it to earth. Fear of not having enough faith is no longer an obstacle. You have faith and you have the ability to live and move in both worlds.

You have God's faith. Believe the mountain in your life moves when you speak to it. You have what's needed to take what's in heaven and bring to earth. You need nothing else. What you have is more than enough. You have been authorized to do it. That's what Jesus made available to us. Just do it and hold fast to your confession.

Think about this. When God created the earth it was perfect. God was well pleased with His creation. There was no sin in the earth when it was created. Everything was perfect.

Everything operated according to purpose in its creation. Sin is disobedience to God. When Adam disobeyed God, it was sin which created sickness into the earth as a result. We all agree sickness came into the earth because of sin. Sickness is the result of sin. Jesus removed our sin on the cross. When sin was removed, sickness was removed as well by Jesus's stripes. That's why the Word says we were healed. Sin and sickness are still in the world but it has nothing in me. It no longer has me in bondage or under its control. Therefore sickness no longer has me in bondage or under its control. I don't get sick. It's not in my DNA. I am not susceptible to any sickness or disease. This revelation causes healing to manifest in your body.

CHAPTER 9

The Cross

We all know about the cross, but do we know the cross? Have we truly come face-to-face with the cross? Crucifixion by the Romans was the most hideous way the worse criminals were executed. The execution was public, painful, and shameful. It was to deter other people from becoming criminals. In the Jewish law, death by hanging on a tree was significant because it meant that person was cursed (Deuteronomy 21:23).

The sinless creator who came to earth in the form of man was stripped, beaten mercilessly, beard plucked, spit on, thorns placed on His head as a crown, hung on a tree (cross), then stabbed with a spear on His side. Why would He do it? Why? Why would He submit Himself to such evils (Hebrews 12:2)? Why would He allow them or us to do that to Him? It was all about love. This type of love cannot be explained or taught. It has to be revealed. It is not of this earth. It's beyond this fallen world. It is beyond understanding. His love for us was greater than the pain and humiliation.

God's love surpasses human love, knowledge, and understanding. His love can only be known and understood by dying to live it. In this love, there is no guilt or condemnation, no judgment or hate. It's pure. It's clean. It's for everyone, and there are a host of people who have it and have it on.

Adam's sin made everyone that came out of his loins sinners. Adam's sin separated everyone from God, their creator. If you've ever created anything and it was good, you don't want to lose it. Everything God made was good, and now His enemy had control of it and all that accompanied it. He now controlled man. The only way He could eternally get it back was to pay the redemption price. God paid the redemptive price by giving His son, which was the ultimate act of love. Jesus paid the price by giving His life for ours.

The price for sin had to be paid. Jesus, the spotless Lamb of God, was given for the sins of humanity. He was the only qualified person to do so. The way it was done was when Jesus the perfect, spotless Lamb of God, hung on that tree; and even before He hung on the tree, in the garden of Gethsemane, He submitted Himself to the plan of the Father. The plan was His arrest to the Roman authorities for the sake of Israel and the world. He was tortured, humiliated and crucified. On the surface it seemed like the devil had won. He finally found the one who God said would "bruise his head." He had gotten rid of him, or so he thought. He had crucified his only threat. He was dead and gone. Unknown to satan was Jesus's death was God's plan, not man's nor his. There was more to come.

The cross was the place where the price for sin was paid which led to the removal of God's wrath. Sin opened the door to sickness and disease. When the price of sin was paid, sickness, disease, and all that go with it were removed. Not only was sin dealt with on the cross but also the results of sin (i.e., sickness, disease, anxiety, weakness, affliction, grief, childbirth pain, and pains).

Once sin is removed, healing is guaranteed. Isaiah 53:4–5 says, "Truly, our sicknesses He Himself bore and our sorrows (pain) He carried; yet we thought His troubles were His own fault; but He was severely struck by God. He was wounded for our rebellion; He was crushed for our evil perversion. The rebuke for our peace (shalom) was upon Him. He took our punishment and that made us whole."

All the things Jesus experienced on the cross were natural and supernatural, done by man naturally, and by God spiritually. The Bible says it pleased the Lord to crush Him (Isaiah 53:10). What happened to Him on the cross? If you believe and accept, it guarantees you right standing with God; in other words, God is now your Father. You are no longer a sinner. You are no longer an enemy of God. He treats you as His very own because you are: healing, divine health, prosperity and supernatural peace all the time. The word *peace* in Hebrew is *shalowm*. It means to be safe (in mind, body or estate), well, healthy, prosperity, peace, happy, favor and complete. This is a simple compilation of words used to define *shalam*.

The cross is known as the double cure. The solution for sin and sickness is found at the cross. Isaiah 53 is a prophecy Jesus fulfilled. It's a description of the savior of the world. The arm of the Lord is Jesus. He was revealed to many in His day as the Messiah, through His teachings, healings, wisdom, signs, wonders, and miracles. When Jesus, the Son of God, hung on the cross, it was not just for salvation of the spirit—it was for salvation of the body as well. Salvation of the body is healing and divine health.

Galatians 3:13 states, "Christ hath redeemed us from the curse of the law, having become a curse for us: (for it is written, cursed is everyone who hangs on a tree." Christ rescued us from the curse we were under because we had broken God's law. Sin is the breaking of God's law. No one was ever able to keep the law since Adam sinned. Sin was in his blood; therefore, all were dead to God because of the sin in the blood. Therefore, no man was qualified to redeem man. The hopelessness of humanity caused God to step in to deliver His creation. The significance of the qualification of the deliverer not breaking the law is that if He broke the law, he was also under the same condemnation of God's wrath; therefore, he would be unable to draw near to God. His blood would be tainted. He would not be the "spotless lamb" (1 Peter 1:19). He would be unable to draw near to God as the sacrifice as well as the High Priest who would have to take the sacrifice to heaven. That's why God sent Jesus in the form of man. He laid aside His heavenly wealth and glory, and came to earth in the form of man.

That's why we love Jesus so much and desire His presence so much. He was the only qualified person. He gave up everything to redeem us and to be the faithful high priest we needed. He left His glory behind and became poor so we could share in His glory. He became the curse so we could be in right standing with God. In other words, we are no longer bound or hounded by judgment because

Jesus, the son of God, set us free from the curse when He became the curse.

You might be saying, *I haven't sinned*. Romans 3:23 says, "For all have sinned and fallen short of the glory of God." It's in your DNA. For the believer, Jesus set us free from sin. We have the power of God resident in us to not sin if we choose. For us, sin is a choice. Romans 6:14 also says, "For sin shall not have dominion over you; for you are not under the law, but under grace."

Dominion means "lord." Sin doesn't have lordship over us because we live under grace when we made Jesus the Lord over our lives. Sin has no control over us. In addition the Word of God says, "If we walk in the light as He is in the light, we have fellowship one with another, and the blood of Jesus Christ, His Son, cleanses (this is continuous action of the blood working) us from all unrighteousness (1 John 1:7)."

Repent and turn your heart totally to Him. Leave the world behind. The world entices you into itself which leads to sin. Turn to Jesus, the Word made flesh, and experience a new life of health.

CHAPTER 10

The Resurrection

Jesus was crucified as a criminal. The powers that be were thrilled about it. They all thought it was His end. But little did they know that His crucifixion was a major part of the plan. God gave Adam authority to rule and reign in the earth when He created him (Genesis 1:26, 28). When Adam sinned, he was not only separated from God, but he also gave satan his authority to rule and reign in the earth.

God gave Adam two sets of instructions, the first consisted of three parts: dominion over everything, replenish the earth, and subdue it. The second instruction was to cultivate and keep the garden of Eden (Genesis 2:15). The garden of Eden was the place from which Adam was to rule and reign. That was the place he met God. God told Adam to rule over everything. Adam's loss of authority is also confirmed when satan tempts Jesus to worship him in exchange for the authority and the glory that was given to him by Adam. This is in reference to what happened when Adam ate of the tree of the knowledge of good and evil. In addition, a very enlightening scripture is Psalm 115:16, "The heaven, even the heavens, are the Lord's: but the earth hath He given to the children of men."

I see the garden of Eden being similar to my sitting room. That's where God and I meet every day, and nothing interferes with that place or the time we meet. I work very hard to keep every distraction out of that place and the time we meet. That's where we come together and where I am reminded we are one. It's a special place.

It's a precious place. It's a holy place. That's the place where I pour out my love on Him and it's the place where He engulfs me with His presence. This is the place, in His Presence, where symptoms cannot manifest, so they just flee.

Even though Jesus went to the cross for our sins and the results of sin, there was additionally something else that needed to happen. To restore man back to his place in the earth of ruling and reigning, something else needed to happen. The devil nor his demons saw what was going to happen next.

Every demon and fallen spirit including satan was partying because the one who could destroy them was—they thought—destroyed. Jesus, their threat was removed or so they thought. Jesus needed to go to hell to complete the work for all humanity for eternity. He bore our sins. He didn't have any of His own. Our sins, sicknesses, diseases, and what the Father did to Him killed Him. "Satan thought it was his plan to kill Jesus using the Roman government and the religious establishment of the day. But he was so wrong. Isaiah 53:10 states, "Yet it pleased the Lord to bruise Him; He has put Him to grief. When You make His soul an offering for sin, He shall see His seed, He shall prolong His days, and the pleasure of the Lord shall prosper in His hand..." Because of our sins, He was separated from God. The devil probably thought when the Father was bruising Jesus and putting Him to grief it was because of Jesus breaking the law. But Jesus never broke the law. The scribes and Pharisees accused Him of breaking the law; but instead He fulfilled it. What they saw as punishment for breaking the law was actually Jesus as the sin offering for humanity.

Deuteronomy 23:22 states, "If a man have committed a sin worthy of death and he be put to death and thou hang him on a tree; his body shall not remain all night upon the tree but thou shalt in any wise bury him that day (for he that is hanged is accursed of God) that thy land be not defiled, which the Lord thy God giveth for an inheritance."

Jesus committed no sin because He had none. It was our sins that were placed on Him. That's how He got to hell to finish eternal salvation for man. Remember hell was made for satan, his cohorts, and those who broke God's law. Jesus did not break God's law. They treated Him like He was cursed by God. In that moment, He was cursed because our sin was placed on Him.

Our sins were the avenue for Jesus to get into Hades. It was all a part of the plan. Hades was the place where satan strategized and made his plans. *Hades*, the Greek word for hell is the place of torment. Hades was the place where the keys were, that Jesus needed to complete the work of salvation for humanity.

Revelation 1:17–18 Jesus says, "Do not be afraid; I am the first and the last, and the living One, and I was dead and look, I am alive forevermore and I have the keys of death and of Hades."

To restore man to God's intent, Jesus needed those keys. Keys represent authority. Those keys locked and unlocked death and Hades. As a believer, you can't die before Jesus says so unless you desire. Hell is locked to the children of God but open to those who choose it. Death is also closed to the children of God until it's their time. The time is determined by you and Jesus. Satan can't kill you unless you choose. Death can't remove you unless you choose. Yes, God knows your days. Knowing your days and choosing your days are different. God doesn't interfere unless you ask Him. The power of choice is very real. You have a will and it is very real. God wouldn't violate your will. But if you want more days you can have it. All you have to do is ask. Remember Hezekiah? You have not because you didn't ask. This is what the cross provided.

Before Christ was raised from the dead, the saints of God stayed in Abraham's bosom which was far above Hell (Luke 16:23). It was necessary that the heavenly things were purified with the blood of Jesus (Hebrews 9:23). When Jesus died, Matthew records the veil of the temple was torn in two from top to bottom. The sacrifice was paid; sin no longer separated man from God because Jesus removed it.

God sent His angel and he tore the veil. Access was now available to the holy of holies by the blood of Jesus. The veil was torn in two, and the Old Testament saints were raised from the dead, seen walking around Jerusalem after Jesus was raised from the dead. They left Abraham's bosom and ascended to heaven because the way was now made through the blood of Jesus. That's why when Jesus rose from the dead and met Mary Magdalene at the sepulcher, He told her to not touch Him because He had not yet ascended to His Father to cleanse the heavenly things. In that blood cleansing of the heavenly things, satan no longer has access to heaven, the throne room of God. He did with Job because Jesus's blood was not yet shed.

Satan can't accuse me anymore before God. So he tries to have us accuse each other. That's where the power of love takes over, choosing to believe the best of everyone. I love the statement penned by Apostle Guillermo Maldonado of King Jesus Ministry from the Holy Spirit. He says, "satan is dethroned, destroyed, disarmed, and defeated."

Jesus's death took Him to the place where He needed to defeat satan permanently which was amongst his cohorts in his territory—hell. In addition, He needed to get those keys of death and Hades. As stated prior, keys are representative of authority to open and close. Death and hell were the last keys He needed to solidify His authority everywhere over everything. Satan has no access to the throne of God anymore. He is locked out of heaven where God resides, and heaven is open to us. The blood of Jesus made sure to that. Now Jesus has all authority in heaven and earth. Nothing is locked to Him. He has the keys to open every door and He has opened every door we need. Matthew 28:18 Jesus says, "All authority has been given to Me in heaven and on earth. Go therefore and make disciples of all the nations…"

God's intent has never changed. It was still His plan for man to have dominion, replenish, and subdue. That's why He needed to go to hell. He needed to take back from satan what Adam relinquished to him. When you have all the keys, you have all the authority. It was never God's intent for man to die. Hell was not created for man. As soon as Adam sinned, his body went from eternal to natural and started deteriorating to the point of death. In other words, there is an expiration date on man's body. Notice the farther away humanity moved from the beginning, man's life span continued to shorten.

Jesus was crucified as a criminal but He wasn't. That's why hell couldn't hold him. It was all a part of the plan. He took our sins on

Himself. He took our sicknesses and diseases as well. Everything that separated us from God, and the results of the separation, Jesus took from us and it was laid on Him. This is powerful if you believe it.

This means you are not a slave to sin any longer. Sin is a choice. This means you were healed. You don't have to die prematurely from any sickness or disease. In fact, you can leave this earth not sick. God said man would return to the ground because man was formed from the ground but He didn't say it would be through sickness or disease. Our physical bodies are all returning to the earth. We choose how we go. This might sound arrogant or unbelievable but it is the truth. Christ has redeemed us from the curse of the law. Sickness and disease were the curse that came on man for breaking the law. Christ changed all that by taking our sickness and disease on the cross. We don't have to die from sickness or disease anymore. We can lay our bodies down.

"The righteous shall blossom like the palm tree; he shall grow like a cedar in Lebanon" (Psalm 92:12). I have experienced two category 5 hurricanes and one thing that always remained standing after they have passed over is the palm tree. And the palm tree looks as beautiful as it did before the hurricane. The cedars of Lebanon take time to grow and they are resilient trees. Cedar is a quality wood, has a pleasant odor and is resistant to rot and insects. That's why it was used so much by the ancient cultures and the Israelites in temple building. It's a very valuable wood. Cedars represent strength and immortality.

Those that are planted in God's house will thrive in His courts. Even when they are of old age, they are still going to be bringing forth fruit; still increasing (Psalm 92:12–15). Hallelujah! They shall be fertile, anointed, and prosperous. Still flourishing. This is us as we continue to age. God does this because He wants the world to see He is righteous and good, and there is no wickedness in Him.

Psalm 91:14–16, the Lord says, because the person that dwells in His secret place delights in Him, He will deliver him and protect him, because he knows His name (honor, character). When that person calls on Him, He will answer him. He will be with him in trouble. He will deliver him and honor Him. We always talk about honoring God, but God also honors those who dwell in His secret place. The Lord will satisfy him with long life and let him see and experience deliverance, health, prosperity, victory. There is nothing better than what the Lord gives, nothing can compare.

This is so important to understand. Just because you don't see anyone walking in the light of it doesn't mean it's not true. One reason we don't see much of this type of living is because it is not taught much. To position yourself to walk in this type of life, you have to hear the truth of God's Word continually and your heart has to always be on God's altar. You can be the first person around your sphere of influence to walk in this truth. The cross and resurrection have removed all limitations and blockages. If you believe it, you can have it. The sky is not the limit. God is and He has no limitations. So what is going to be your excuse for not having it?

CHAPTER 11

The Word of God

Throughout every chapter the Word of God has been the source and key. The word of God reveals who God is. If you want to know who someone really is, listen to the person speak. Their words reveal who they are. Out of the abundance of the heart the mouth speaks. I know God first by what He says, secondly I know Him by experience. The Word actually prepared me for experience. For every miracle and healing I have experienced, the Word was the key.

> The old way with laws etched in stone, led to death, though it began with such glory that the people of Israel could not bear to look at Moses' face. For his face shone with the glory of God, even though the brightness was already fading away. Shouldn't we expect far greater glory under the new way, now that the Holy Spirit is giving life? If the old way, which brings condemnation, was glorious, how much more glorious is the new way, which makes us right with God! In fact that first glory was not glorious at all compared with the overwhelming glory of the new way. So if the old way, which has been replaced, was glorious, how much more glorious is the new, which remains forever! (NLT)

THE TRUTH ABOUT YOUR HEALING

God's Word broke the fear and took my mind off the disease that didn't have power over me because of the cross. Every time my mind went to thinking about a disease, I felt sick. When my mind was on the Word, the sickness had no power over my mind or body. I didn't even know I had a body at those times. The longer I spent in the Word, the healthier my mind became, and there were no more symptoms of the disease, until finally the sickness was gone. I carried years of an unhealthy mind because of sickness. When the symptoms totally left, I didn't immediately recognize it was gone because my mind was on Him and His kingdom.

Based on us living in a fallen world, our unrenewed minds tend to go in the direction of the world. And the enemy hammers it in by trying to have us continually look at the symptoms and name of the disease. When we allow our minds to go in that direction, it creates the symptoms in our body by speaking to our body, then we start feeling the symptoms, even though when our minds were not on the disease or sickness, there were no symptoms. If your mind doesn't go back to symptoms, name of disease, and/or feelings, you know you are healed. The key is not continually going back and rehearsing the symptoms you are expecting to feel. This can only be done by renewing your mind to the Word of God and by the power of the Holy Spirit. This is also the power in true praise and worship. When you are truly in the presence of God, your mind is not on symptoms.

Our rehearsing of symptoms and the name of the disease actually gives the disease power in our lives. Notice that when you start feeling symptoms, it is never full blast. It starts minor. Then it increases as you think about it. Then it tries to take over your mind. At that place where the symptoms are minor, the disease is trying to get a foothold in your body. The disease possibly was developing in your body over a period of time and you never felt anything. Then one day you begin to feel something. At that point, use your lordship over your body and use your authority. Don't allow the spirit speaking to your mind an opportunity to manifest in your body. Don't allow your mind to harvest the evil thoughts which create and increase a disease in your body. Jesus already bore it so you don't have to. For you to allow it back is the same as saying Jesus did not take it from you, and what He did on the cross was not enough for you to walk in health.

Many people never pay attention to the fact that their minds communicate to their bodies and tell their bodies what it is feeling and what it is not. One of the terms used is *talking mind*. Yes, your mind is talking but to whom? When it comes to emotions, feelings in the body, your mind is actually speaking to your body. Sometimes it's a spirit talking through your mind to your body. That's why it's important to renew your mind. Renewing your mind helps remove the "talking mind" whether it's simply the mind speaking based on the world around it at that time or a spirit speaking to your mind.

The Word of God is so powerful that it separates truth and fiction that comes to our minds. It is alive and powerful, and sharper than any two-edged sword, piercing even to the dividing asunder of soul and spirit and of the joints and marrow, and is a discerner of the thoughts and intents of the heart. This is Hebrews 4:12. The Word of God is operative; it is active. It is working all the time when spoken, to bring about the results that are latent in it.

The spoken Word brings about results that changes everything on earth. We are told to take "the sword of the Spirit which is the Word of God." Part of our arsenal of weapons is the Spirit's sword. When we use His sword under His leadership, power is released. In war movies soldiers are told many times when to shoot their guns. In the days of Rome when the Romans were in battle, they used their weapons when commanded by their lead ranking officer above them (i.e., centurion). To be able to use His sword at the right time which is when it will have its greatest impact, you must be led by Him.

The Word of God differentiates between the "talking mind" versus "the Spirit's voice." It clears it up so that you know what direction you are to go. Another way of saying it is the Word of God differentiates between the natural, carnal, fleshy man versus the spirit man. It differentiates between the lower nature versus the God nature; the baser nature from the spiritual nature, the animal mindset from the spiritual mindset. In essence, it distinguishes between the earthy man and the spiritual man. I like the Passion Translation, which says, "For we have the living Word of God, which is full of energy, like a two-mouthed sword. It will even penetrate to the very core of our being where soul and spirit, bone and marrow meet! It interprets and reveals the true thoughts and secret motives of our hearts."

The one whose mind is renewed with the Word of God is the one who will walk as the spiritual man, he is and will be healed. Mind renewal to the Word of God is of utmost importance. This is important because truth, the Word of God, gives freedom, joy, health, peace, and much more.

CHAPTER 12

The Power of Reading the Word Out Loud

The Lord made it very clear to me if I would feed on Him, I would live. And I wanted to live. Jesus's response to the devil when he tempted Him was, "Man shall not live by bread alone, but by every word that comes out of the mouth of God." The Word of God saved me and the Word of God healed me. He wanted me to focus on His Son, to be consumed and overtaken by His Word, not the symptoms. Most people focus on symptoms; but God says focus on Him. Whatever your focus is what controls your life. Stop allowing the spirit of fear to control your life. It does it by reminding you of the symptoms. You might say, *I would if I could, but the pain is overwhelming.* I say to you, *let Him overwhelm you.*

In my greatest time of need—because of the distress and pain—I literally cried to Him and asked Him to help me because the pain was too much, and He came to my rescue. At that point, I was not eloquent in my speech. It was bare bone basic. *God, help me.* You are no different from me if you are born of His Spirit. We have the same DNA because we have the same Father. And our DNA is that of our Father. Every good father will come to his child's rescue especially when in pain. He's no different. He's much, much better than a good or excellent earthly father.

I started reading the Word, specifically the gospels because Jesus is the Word made flesh. This was my assignment from the Lord. My mind needed cleansing. Many years of sickness changes a person.

I would have to say, I didn't know who I was apart from sickness because that was all I knew. My life accommodated the sickness. I needed to know who I truly was created to be.

When I read Matthew, Mark, Luke, and John, I started learning who I was meant to be apart from sickness. For me that was the most important thing. Your need might be something else. It could be always poor, lacking in finances, a slave to the financial system. That changes you. Your mind becomes so occupied with getting out of sickness, getting out of debt. That's where your mind wants to continually run back to, and in so doing, you are always aware of your current situation; and there's nothing to take you to the new real you, unless there is divine intervention.

Who are *you*? Don't give the Christianese. You can't change what you don't like if you don't admit you don't like what you see. Who are *you* from your heart? Don't be a shell parroting what you've been told to say or what you think people want to hear or people would like or what you wish you could be. When you look in the mirror what do you see? A tired scared person or a person carrying the weight of this world? Do you like what you see in the mirror? If you don't, there's another mirror. There's a more accurate mirror. "But we all, with unveiled face, beholding as in a mirror the glory of the Lord, are being transformed into the same image from glory to glory, just as by the Spirit of the Lord" (2 Corinthians 3:18).

The Holy Spirit takes the Word we read and uses it to change us into His image. That's why we need to continue to meditate on the Word of God. We are progressively changed. It progressively changes us into His image as long as we have the desire for change. But notice there must first be an unveiling. Second Corinthians 3:16 in the Amplified New Testament states, "But whenever a person turns (in repentance) to the Lord, the veil is stripped off and taken away. Repentance which is turning to the Lord is the key to the removal of the veil.

The Amplified New Testament further states in verse 18, "And all of us, as with unveiled face, (because we) continued to behold (in the Word of God) as in a mirror the glory of the Lord, are constantly being transfigured into His very own image in ever increasing splendor and from one degree of glory to another; (for this comes) from the Lord (Who is) the Spirit."

In our own personal lives, we need an unveiling. To *unveil* means "to make something secret known; to remove a veil or covering from" (dictionary.cambridge.org, www.merriam-webster.com). The necessity of unveiling is to be truthful to yourself. This is difficult for many people but from that place of truthfulness, lies will be removed and the things you believed that were not true or the things in our cultures that keep us in bondage will be recognized so it can be removed. It's important to come to the truth about who you are, where you are in life, what is lacking, what is needed, and where you are going. Is health lacking? Is peace lacking? Are friendships lacking? Are you always in financial lack? Do you have family issues? Why? What's the cause? Until a person acknowledges the truth of their circumstances, not even God can help. Honesty with God is paramount for His intervention. Once you have experienced an unveiling based on honesty, then truth will stay. Truth remains when there is openness and honesty with Him. The Spirit of God works in and through truth.

The Bible has stories of many people; people who were in need that met Jesus. When they encountered Jesus, they were healed, delivered, and set free. Interesting that there were many people that met Him and were in His presence but weren't delivered.

"Now it happened on a certain day, as He was teaching, that there were Pharisees and teachers of the law sitting by, who had come out of every town of Galilee, Judea, and Jerusalem. And the power of the Lord was present to heal them" (Luke 5:17 NKJV). In this scenario, the man whose friends pushed him to Jesus was healed. The other people around Jesus weren't healed.

I moved from being in the crowd with sickness to one who encountered Him and then to one who walked with Him and helped others encounter Him. Do you want to stay in the crowd or do you want to encounter Him? Walk with Him; you'll be set free. And then bring others to walk alongside Him. Every one of us makes the choice. Make the right choice which is to move from the crowd to the one who is totally transformed because of a personal unveiling.

I was on the other side, sick and tired of being sick, and tired and angry with the world. Now I am on Jesus's side. You can as well. Jesus's side is administering His love, life, fire, and deliverance.

I'll never forget a business woman once asked me if I believed I was successful. I didn't have anything at that time. I wasn't married. Was in the ministry for a few years. I didn't have a house. I lived with my parents. I thought it was a strange question because she had the things I didn't. If I was under the hypnotic spell of the world, I would have said no. But I wasn't. I had something the world couldn't give and that was Jesus, the Savior-King. With Him I don't need anything, and with Him I have everything.

I lived in the gospel for a long season. I read the gospels out loud every day. Matthew was on Monday; Mark was Tuesday; Luke was Wednesday and John was Thursday. Reading the gospels over and over out loud every day, something happened on the inside of me. Power was inside me that I didn't know I had. I was filled with the Holy Spirit and spoke in other tongues for years, but something happened when I fed on the gospels daily. I had power I didn't experience before. I stopped thinking about the sickness. I was refreshed from the exhaustion of fighting in my own strength, thinking I was operating out of His strength.

To feed on Him means to meditate and spend time in His presence. Just like you have to eat food to live; so it is in the realm of God where healing, prosperity, peace, debt breaking, joy can be found. If you eat three meals a day to survive and feel good physically, think about your spirit self. How do you treat your spirit self? Do you memorize Scripture? Do you sit down, read the word, and ponder what you read? Do you speak the word in your mind? That is feeding. When you have done all those things, you can say you have been feeding on the Word of God.

God told Joshua to be strong and very courageous; be observant to do all that is written in the law. If he, Joshua, doesn't turn from it to go to the right or to the left, he would be successful wherever he went. Then the Lord reiterated to him again but in more details. He said to him, the Word was not to depart from his mouth. He was to meditate on it day and night so that he would be careful to do all that is written in it. When he does that then he, Joshua, makes his way prosperous, and he would have success. Then God commands him again to be strong and courageous. He also commands him to not be afraid because He would be with him wherever he went. This is feeding. When that is done every sickness, every disease, every demon of oppression and depression, every fear, all poverty—leaves.

Unfortunately, many times we miss full deliverance because we look for the hands of a man to bring deliverance because we are too busy to go to God for it ourselves, and all the time God is beckoning us to come to Him. God has a hand. His hand is His word and the Spirit, both of whom are waiting for us. I have been healed many times, by a man empowered by God, herbs or supplements, and by fellowship with Him around His Word.

The one I love the most, and beginning to find to be the easiest way to receive is by fellowship with Him around the Word. I love the wake-up call that He's waiting for us to get together more intimately. I love being on my knees, on my couch wrapped in a blanket acknowledging *here I am Lord*, just like Samuel responded after hearing Him but not recognizing His voice the first two times. He got it the third time. That's the way it is with many. He calls and we don't hear or misread what's being said. But when your resolve is you are going to stick with it until you recognize Him, you always do, and healing always comes. One way or the other, He makes the way for you to get it.

Heaven and earth will pass away, but His Word will not pass away. It's eternal, which means it has the power in it to sustain itself, which means it will do what it says. Even if you have given up on everything, don't give up on the Word of God. With patience and perseverance, you will reap what you have sown. If you sow the Word, you'll have the results of the Word.

I remember the story of a man who wouldn't speak God's Word over himself. He would attend church once in a while. He heard the Word taught and preached. His family were believers. His family prayed; the leadership prayed. Everyone encouraged him to say what God said about him, to speak the Word of God over his body using scriptures like 1 Peter 2:24 and Isaiah 53:5. His response was he would be lying if he said he was healed because he wasn't. The power of calling those things that be not as though they were, was ministered to him. It was explained to him he wasn't lying; he was simply saying what God said. He spoke other things but not what God said. He had a stroke and totally lost his ability to speak. Basically this man got what he said and more.

God told Joshua the Word was not to depart from his mouth. That's the same exhortation to us today. Do not let the Word of God depart from your mouth. If the Word of God isn't coming out of your mouth, something else is or nothing (like the man with the stroke), and both those conditions are not good.

CHAPTER 13

Invasion

Sicknesses and diseases that infect the body are an invasion into the cells and DNA of man's body. Viruses that contaminate the body are from the outside moving into the body. They live outside the body. Once in the body they start to multiply. They become alive. Viruses are like demons. They live outside of human beings but once they get inside they multiply and start to take over and affect the body. "Viruses cannot replicate unless absorbed by cells in our body. Once a virus is outside the body, its capsid starts to degrade, and the more degraded its capsid is, the less likely it is to survive. When outside the body, these capsids degrade faster in cold dry environments" (covid19.nj.gov>about-the-virus).

Capsid is the protein shell or outer layer of a virus that surrounds its genetic material. Scientist say technically viruses are not alive. In God's world, anything that multiplies has life. Only life can multiply; nothing else. Inside our bodies is the environment they need to live. Jesus changed that. Our bodies' DNA strand is different. I proclaim my DNA is from my Father. My Father is God. He doesn't get sick; neither does His first born who is Jesus. Therefore, I do not get sick because I am second, third, etc. born. I declare my body is not the breathing ground for viruses because my DNA is not susceptible to viruses, cancers, organ failures. This is all a part of our inheritance as children of God.

Everything created has the ability to hear. It might not be able to hear your voice but it can hear its creator's voice. Remember everything God created was very good. There is a barrier God made in creation that separates man from animal. The creatures were actually made to work for Adam. They were not equivalent to him in the creation. He was to rule and reign over them. He was to reign and rule through his voice. Through Adam's sin, the ability to rule and reign was lost. Creation was put under the death sentence of depravity and emptiness. It was in bondage; no longer able to communicate with man. Like Cain and Abel, creation started doing the same thing; killing each other, fighting for power, scavenging and killing for food.

Through Jesus, man was restored to his place of authority to reign and rule. Ruling and reigning is done through Christ and with Christ. All of creation is waiting for the sons of God to be revealed (Romans 8:19–23). In that revealing will come creation's obedience. Even nature is waiting to hear the sons of God. The winds, the seas, everything is waiting for the sons of God. Jesus walked on water because He is the firstborn Son of God. He was obedient to the Father. The winds and the sea listened to His command because they recognized His voice. Creation responds to the sons of God because they are the voice of God in the earth (Matthew 8:25–26).

Verse 27 of Matthew 8 states, "But the men marveled, saying, what manner of man is this, that even the winds and the sea obey him!" At this point the disciples didn't recognize what was happening. God was preparing them to do the same thing by showing them what was possible. Jesus is the first born as stated in Colossians 1:15, 18. Romans 8:29 makes it emphatically clear that Jesus is the firstborn among many brethren. If there is a firstborn, then there is a second born and third born.

CHAPTER 14

Immunity

There's a place in God we have because of the cross that many have not heard about or don't believe. We sometimes touch on it based on Isaiah 53:4–5 and 2 Peter 2:24. One of the things I have learned about God is that there are no limits for us if we believe. Our Father has no limits; He is God. We have no limits because we are children of God.

After the children of Israel crossed the Red Sea and the Egyptians were swallowed up in the sea, the first covenant God made with Israel is Exodus 15:26. God made a statute and an ordinance for the people. This happened after they complained about not having good water to drink. They get to Marah and the water is healed so it's drinkable. He told them at Marah, "If they would carefully listen to His voice and do what He told them to do, obeying the commands and keeping His decrees, they would not suffer any of the diseases that Egypt experienced because He was the Lord their healer. God makes this agreement with Israel that they would not have any of the diseases the Egyptians had, Egypt being a type of the world. God became their healer.

Later on, Moses goes to Mount Sinai to receive the commandments of the Lord for Israel. He gives Moses the commandments, rules and laws for the people to live by. At that time God also reconfirmed His healing arrangement with them. He tells Moses they were to serve Him, and He would bless their bread and water, and He would remove sickness from their midst. No one would miscarry or be barren in their land, and they would fully live out their days. Basically what the Lord was saying was they would live long healthy lives if they served Him. He would turn off sicknesses from them. Such great promises they had.

Joshua is about to take Moses' place. The children of Israel are preparing to start the trek into the promised land. Before Moses leaves, he reiterates the history, the laws, the commandments and statutes of the first generation that left Egypt but not entered into the promised land because of rebellion. On Mount Gerizim, Moses reminds them that if they were careful to obey the Lord, do His commandments—which he, Moses, gave them—the Lord would do marvelous things for them. So the blessings the first generation were given also applied to their children under the same terms and conditions.

Generally speaking, the body of Christ is living far below the benefits of the cross. Psalm 103:3 says, "Bless the Lord O my soul and all that is within me, bless His holy name. Bless the Lord O my soul and forget not all His benefits." He tells us not to forget what we know; but there is still much we don't know that we definitely need to learn about such as immunity. The work Jesus did on the cross is more powerful than many people realize. To have the inheritance of immunity is incomprehensible to most. That's just like our God. He always goes far beyond our hopes, dreams, imaginations (Ephesians 3:20). If I am immune then I don't worry about having any kind of disease or sickness. Is it possible to live in immunity? The children of Israel weren't only healed when they needed it but they also had immunity. The healing was necessary when they disobeyed the Lord. They walked in immunity as long as they obeyed Him.

Immunity is defined as exemption or resistance. If you're protected against something, you have immunity to it. In a medical sense, immunity is "protection from disease" (https://www.vocabulary.com.dictionary). One of the benefits of the new covenant is immunity. However, the idea of immunity first appears in the Old Covenant. "If thou wilt diligently hearken to the voice of the Lord thy God and wilt do that which is right in his sight and wilt give ear to His commandments and keep all His statutes, I will put none of these diseases upon thee which I have brought upon the Egyptians: for I am the Lord that healeth thee" (Exodus 15:26).

Another way of stating Exodus 15:26 is if you will be diligent in listening and doing the word of the Lord, you would be protected from diseases. Diseases nor sickness would have access or entry into your life because there'll be supernatural protection. You would be protected. Supernatural protection is our inheritance. Exodus 15:26 is where God establishes Himself as the healer for all the nation of Israel.

The Lord repeats a second time to Israel in Exodus 23:25–26, "And ye shall serve the Lord your God and He shall bless thy bread and thy water and I will take sickness away from the midst of thee. There shall nothing cast their young, nor be barren, in thy land: the number of thy days I will fulfill."

The words *I will take* mean to turn off, take off, turn away, behead, put (away, down) just to list a few. God turned off sickness and disease from the nation of Israel once they obeyed Him. It's amazing what the Lord did for the children of Israel and what He does for all His children who know Him.

Deuteronomy 7, Israel is warned again if they keep, take heed; and do His commandments, statutes and judgments, He would keep His covenant and His lovingkindness to them. In other words, what He promised their forefathers He would be obliged to do for them. One of the things the Lord would do is in verse 15. He would remove all sickness and He would not put on them any of the diseases of Egypt which they knew and feared (Deuteronomy 28:60), but instead He would put it on those who hate them. Not even Balaam, the prophet, who was hired by Balak to curse Israel could accomplish such a task. Every time he opened his mouth, he blessed Israel. How can anyone curse whom God has blessed (Numbers 23:8)? It's impossible! This is part of the blessing for you as well. It doesn't matter what title a person carries. They cannot curse who God has blessed, and God has blessed His children.

Deuteronomy is known as the second law. In Deuteronomy 8, Moses rehearses to the children of Israel how the Lord dealt with them. He also gives them specific instructions so they would experience the blessings God ordained for them. One of the things Moses mentions is the fact that they walked through *the great and terrible wilderness*, where there was very deadly serpents, scorpions, and no water nor rain. The only time they were bitten by serpents was when they spoke against God and Moses. That was when the supernatural protection was lifted. They didn't realize the nation as a whole was walking in the supernatural power of God.

It's the same today. When we speak evil against the Holy Spirit like they did, we remove the supernatural protection of God and there are consequences. Even when we speak against those carrying the anointing of God which is the body of Christ, we align ourselves with evil and receive the results of it. If you are seeking God for healing, stay aligned with God. Nothing stops healing more than the use of the tongue in a negative way. First Peter 3:10–12 says, "He who would love life and see good days, let him refrain his tongue from evil and his lips from speaking deceit. Let him turn away from evil and do good; let him seek peace and pursue it. For the eyes of the Lord are on the righteous and His ears are open to their prayers; but the face of the Lord is against those who do evil."

Imagine walking in the wilderness that didn't have water nor rain forty years, and your feet don't swell. That's supernatural. Their shoes nor clothes wore out. The same shoes for forty years through the *terrible wilderness*. It's unheard of. Deuteronomy 34:7 says, "And Moses was a hundred and twenty years old when he died: his eyes were not dim, nor his natural force abated. In other words, Moses wasn't blind nor was he weak when he died. He was strong physically. You might think that was because Moses saw the Lord. Moses saw the back parts of God which revealed His glory. Second Corinthians 3:7 from the New Living Translation say, "The old way, with laws etched in stone, led to death, though it began with such glory that the people of Israel could not bear to look at Moses' face. For his face shone with the glory of God, even though the brightness was already fading away."

Ephesians 2:5–6 states, "Even when we were dead in sins, hath He quickened us together with Christ, (by grace ye are saved) and hath raised us up together and made us sit together in heavenly places in Christ Jesus." Seated in heavenly places in Christ is the position where immunity works. Nothing can touch you in that place.

Psalm 91 is a confirming scripture. Verse 1 is the person who dwells in the secret place of the most high shall live under the shadow of the Almighty. In that place He becomes your shelter and castle. You can't be reached or touched from that position. You are immune. Psalm 91 is a great Psalm on immunity. Another great Psalm is 103. "Bless the Lord O my soul and forget not all His benefit; who forgiveth all thine iniquities; who healeth ALL, (not some) thy diseases."

We have been blessed by God who is Jesus's Father with all spiritual blessings in heavenly places in Christ. As long as we are in that place we are immune. Remember we are living in the risen one. No disease or sickness can penetrate the resurrection power of the Lord Jesus Christ.

Plagues and pestilences are a result of man in rebellion to God. This is consistent with scriptures. Whenever God's people were in rebellion they faced crisis. Then they repented, and God gave them a deliverer. The only deliverer who has the ability to deliver in every situation is the creator, Jesus.

Deuteronomy 28 lists all the curses of breaking the law. They are pestilence (plagues), tuberculosis, fever, inflammation, extreme burning, botch (ulcer, boils of Egypt), tumor in the anus or pudenda, scurvy, itching that can't be healed. They would be struck with madness (craziness), blindness, heart problems, oppression, problems in the knees and legs, sores that cannot be healed from the sole of the feet to the top of the head. All these physical diseases would come upon them until they were destroyed. If they didn't do the words of the law which would lead them to reverence and honor the Lord and His name, all the diseases of Egypt that they were afraid of would cling to them and every sickness and every disease, every plague not written in the book of the law would come upon them until they were destroyed. But Galatians 3:13 also confirms immunity. "Christ has redeemed us from the curse of the law, being made a curse for us; for it is written, cursed is everyone that hangeth on a tree that the blessing of Abraham might come on the Gentiles through Jesus Christ; that we might receive the promise of the Spirit through faith."

Diseases and sicknesses are the curse that comes as a result of breaking the law. In other words if the law is not broken then there is no sickness or disease. Every disease listed as well as not listed, known as well as not known, Christ has paid the price for us breaking the law by actually becoming the curse for us. In other words, every curse listed above, the anointed one lost His anointing because He became the curse for us so we wouldn't get any sicknesses or disease. Jesus became the curse; we became anointed. Because of what Jesus did, it is as if we never broke God's law.

Egypt is a type of the world. The diseases of the world would overtake Israel if they failed to observe to do the law. The world has nothing in us; therefore, the diseases in the world have nothing in us. What or who we have within us is the Holy Spirit. Unless you know and believe this truth you will constantly be battling the diseases in the world. That's the enemies' desire. Distraction through diseases that are not yours nor were ordained to be yours.

The Israelites were even afraid of the diseases that were in the world. The Lord told them the diseases of the world that they were afraid of would come upon them if they didn't *observe to do all the words of this law that are written in this book*. That's immunity. Doing the Word created the antibodies against the diseases and sicknesses. The dictionary says "antibodies bind to stop it from replicating and also tag viruses so that other blood cells know to destroy them" (www.bbc.co.uk>science).

The foundation that establishes immunity is prophesied throughout Genesis to Malachi. What transpired on the cross is found in Isaiah 53, Galatians 3:13, and 1 Peter 2:24. The cross is the greatest mystery and untapped event in history. We all know we have broken God's law. But praise the Lord, Jesus took the penalty and the results of breaking the law which was all our sicknesses and diseases. Jesus was cursed with our sicknesses and diseases which was due to breaking God's law. If He was cursed with the diseases and sicknesses that were personally ours, we do not have to accept any of them. The power of sickness and disease was removed from us over two thousand years ago when He hung on the cross. Don't be a participant in satan's lying schemes by taking ownership to something that was removed from you over two thousand years ago.

It is not yours. He is a liar, and he's lying.

If you already have a disease or sickness how do get this immunity? The Word has already established you already have immunity. You are not experiencing immunity because you don't know you have it. You have been perishing for lack of knowledge in your health. Your health has been perishing because of a lack of knowledge. Careful study of the word reveals it was made available at the cross. Salvation was made available at the cross. Healing was made available at the cross. Peace was made available at the cross. Immunity was made available at the cross.

Why do you take it in your body when Jesus already moved it from you onto Himself before you were born, so you wouldn't have to bare it? Galatians 3:13 establishes immunity. He already removed every sickness and disease from you over two thousand years ago when He hung on that tree. Don't be a participant in satan's lying schemes.

If the nation of Israel had protection from diseases based on their obedience under the covenant they had with the Lord, how much more the church of the Lord Jesus Christ.

Hebrews 8:6 states that Jesus is the mediator of a better covenant which was established on better promises. Think about this. Hebrews 9:13–15 in the Passion Translation reads,

> Under the old covenant the blood of bulls, goats and the ashes of a heifer were sprinkled on those who were defiled and effectively cleansed them outwardly from their ceremonially impurities. Yet how much more will the sacred blood of the Messiah thoroughly cleanse our consciences! For by the power of the eternal Spirit He has offered Himself to God as the perfect Sacrifice that now frees us from our dead works to worship and serve the living God.

So Jesus is the One who has enacted a new covenant with a new relationship with God so that those who accept the invitation will receive the eternal inheritance He has promised to His heirs. For He died to release us from the guilt of the violations committed under the first covenant.

The first covenant was based on the blood of goats, bulls, and the ashes of heifer cleansing their bodies from ceremonial impurity. Under this covenant, they were able to walk in health as long as they did the word of the Lord. They still had the consciousness of sin. The blood of animals only covered over the sin. The problem was it was not perfectly dealt with because the Messiah had not been crucified. But under the new covenant, Jesus's blood, the spotless Lamb of God, purifies the conscience from dead works so we can worship the living God.

How do you get this immunity? See it in the cross. Believe what Jesus did on the cross was true. Believe that what He did was for you. Believe it's part of your inheritance. If God is willing to give you His Spirit as a down payment of full redemption, why would He not give you immunity as part of redemption? Meditate on the cross and build your relationship with Him.

CHAPTER 15

God's Perfect Expression of Himself!

Jesus is God's perfect expression for healing. If you want to see God's heart, look at Jesus. "Hath in these last days spoken unto us by his Son, whom He hath appointed heir of all things, by whom also He made the worlds; who being the brightness of His glory and the express image of His person and upholding all things by the word of His power" (Hebrews 1:2–3).

Jesus is the exact copy of God. Jesus is the copy of God. When Jesus came to earth He laid aside all His glory which is what makes Him God and came in the form of man. He submitted Himself to death, that is death on the cross. Because of His obedience to death, God elevated Him to the highest position in the seen and unseen world.

One of the most powerful revelations I got from the Lord is that throughout eternity there is now representation of humanity on the throne of God. Before there was none. There was only God as seen in Genesis 1:26. It's interesting to note that Genesis 1:26 and 1:27 are different. God said in verse 26, "Let us make man in our image, after our likeness and let them have dominion over the fish of the sea and over the fowl of the air." Verse 27 says, "So God created man in His own image, in the image of God created him, male and female created them."

Man made in God's image was man representing God in the earth. He had the ability to have dominion. In other words man could subjugate, rule over what was on the earth. In His likeness means man had God's nature. In other words, man would rule and have dominion by love. We sometimes use the term spitting image of a person. That means you look just like the person; but when we say someone is like their parent, it refers to mannerisms, behavior, character. Image is more appearance, and likeness is more mannerisms.

Jesus was made in God's image and likeness. Jesus told His disciples in John 14:7, "If you had known Me, you would have known My Father also; and from now on you know Him and have seen Him." Philip then asked Jesus to show them the Father and they would be satisfied. Jesus's response was "Have I been with you so long and yet you have not known Me, Philip? He who has seen Me has seen the Father; so how can you say, 'Show us the Father'? Do you not believe that I am in the Father and the Father in Me? The words that I speak to you I do not speak on My own authority; but the Father who dwells in Me does the works. Believe Me that I am in the Father and the Father in Me, or else believe Me for the sake of the works themselves."

Whatever anyone wants to know about the Father, all they have to do is look at Jesus His Son. No one on earth was ever a perfect representation of the Father; only Jesus. This is important because God makes it clear the only way to know Him is through His Son, no exception. If you believe that, then what the Son did when He walked the earth—all those who believe will be able to do the same things He did.

In looking at Jesus's obedience to the Father, He humbled Himself to the death of the cross. In His obedience, man's sin was removed from him. The cross was the place where God dealt with sin. Under the Old Covenant, sin was covered over; it was never dealt with at the root. There was always the reminder of sin.

The removal of sin happened as a result of Jesus's death, burial, and resurrection. One act of humility by the last Adam changed the course of humanity forever. Man's fate after he sinned was total separation from God forever. The soul that sins shall die (Ezekiel 18:4). Adam's disobedience brought sin into the world; sin leads to death. But by Jesus's obedience, many were made righteous.

CHAPTER 16

Supernatural Healing Methods

Anointed Vessel

For over 20 years I have known a minister by the name of Frederick Clark. He is a true seer. I use the term seer because it accurately describes him. In ministry his motto is *music, ministry, miracles*. He plays bluegrass Christian music, then he ministers the word of the Lord; and then the miracles. He chooses a person then he starts from the top of the person's head and tells him every sickness or disease he sees. Sometimes he starts from the bottom of their feet and works his way up, depending on what he sees. He doesn't need your help to know your problem and he makes it very clear. He tells you everything he sees and then he might use the microphone or say a very simple prayer, or command you to do something and you are healed.

Over the past twenty years I have never seen him miss it. And there is absolutely no hype. By the time he's through with you, you are healed. Night after night this is how he ministers to people. He also ministers corporately based on the number of people and or diseases or sicknesses he sees the people carrying. When he ministers to a person about ministry, he tells the person his or her name. I have actually seen him spell out unusual names because they were hard to pronounce or foreign to him.

He has been in the ministry now over sixty years. He and his wife have a family of eleven children; two sets of twins. I asked him,

"Why so many children?" His response was the Lord promised him and his wife a girl. His last set of twins are the girls he and his wife were promised. The power of persistence that's found in faith.

Frederick Clark was on the tail end of the voice of healing ministers with Gordon Lindsey, Kenneth Hagin, William Branham, Oral Roberts. He ministers like William Branham. In fact, he relates the story of the person who was in line to receive William Branham's anointing, but refused it because he said, "It was too hard, too difficult a price to pay." When the minister responded to him no, he didn't want it, Frederick Clark asked if he could have it; the minister said yes. Now Frederick Clark, affectionately known as Freddy Clark, ministers like William Branham. And he is very sound doctrinally.

He has been coming every year to our church and every year he comes, there is something fresh and new for everyone because, as the Lord told him, "Every day we wake up, it's a new day with new problems." One year he showed us a Polaroid picture of himself. In the background of the picture, there were two other men that looked like him. He had been asking the Lord who the two people were in the picture with him, and the Lord told him they were revelation and miracles. The two work together to produce healings and miracles.

This entire book can be filled with hundreds of thousands of testimonies of people being healed under his ministry and I have witnessed many over the years. His experiences with the Lord and in ministry have stretched my faith and the possibilities that exists in the Lord. Whenever he comes to our church, I love the time we spend together. I learn things of and in the spirit that would take me years either to experience or to learn on my own.

The last time he was at our church, he ministered to a lady and used the word "immunity." My spirit grabbed hold of the word immunity and the Lord started teaching me about immunity, and that it was given through the cross to His people. This is what separates the world from the church and causes the world to want what the church has.

Brother Clark as we affectionately call him, said he asked the Lord about healing people. The Lord's response was when people are healed, it becomes difficult for them to return to the world. The miracle healing holds them. I remember a lady coming to one of our services one evening. He picked her out and prayed for her state of mind. I don't recall him specifically calling out the disease but he prayed for her healing and told her she would be alright. She was healed. I found out the following day that the same night she came to our church she was diagnosed with breast cancer. She is alive today and doesn't have cancer. This is over twelve years.

He's performed hundreds possibly thousands of surgeries spiritually; thereby, cancelling surgeries that were scheduled. I have seen him pray for people that were anemic. He gives them a spiritual injection and in some cases their faces turn blush from the shot of spiritual blood. He says he does what he sees the angel do; the surgeries, the shots. Many people with knee problems have been healed. Back problems, eye problems healed. If he chooses you, you are healed. If he doesn't call you out and you go to him, he still tells you what's wrong and he does what he needs to and you are healed. It's amazing. He's been a well-kept secret to the body of Christ.

The word of knowledge and the word of wisdom work together hand in hand in the ministry God gave him. The knowledge is what is wrong with the person but the wisdom is what command to give the person that connects them to their healing miracle. One of his greatest desires and prayers to the Lord is "That not one word he speaks falls to the ground (1 Samuel 3:19)" and God has honored him.

If all the testimonies of healings just from our church were written, it would take volumes. The amazing thing is he comes back year after year and ministers to many of the same people, and it is either something new that developed after he left or they were unable to keep their healing. And God still heals them. God doesn't get upset with us. He doesn't judge us. He loves us and wants us well. We have greater impact when we are well.

The gifts of the Spirit or manifestations of the Spirit like most things in our lives as believers has to be developed. They are in a seed form. When you use the gift as opportunity and need arises, it grows and becomes perfected. You were a seed then a baby before you were an adult. You were fed, nurtured, educated, trained to become the adult you are. It's the same with the gifts of the Spirit. They operate differently through different people because we are all different. However, it's the same Spirit.

Gifts of Healing

An amazing phenomenon I learned about many of the ministers in the voice of healing days was that several of the ministers who were a part of the voice of healings each had specific gifts to heal specific diseases. Think about being in a meeting with some of those ministers together. One had an anointing for deafness, another for blindness, another for cancer, another for deliverance. Truly, the body of Christ at work together. It would be spectacular to get some of the ministers with specific anointing's of this day together in one meeting. I believe God would be so pleased because it is a representation of the body of Christ working the gifts together He has given each one of them to heal His body as well as those outside. Great things are happening in this day and age.

Today I see the same operations but with churches more so than a particular person. I know of one church who seems to get people healed with mind and brain problems. Another ministry is known for raising the dead. How are you known? How is your church known? Think about a community filled with the gifts of the Spirit to heal or create new organs for those in the community with a need. It is possible. It is doable. This is what the kingdom of God longs to see. We are on the precipice. Whole communities healed because of the gifts or manifestations of the Spirit for every need.

God works outside the boxes people create. He takes the foolish things of this world to confound the wise. Jerusalem was in good confusion after the outpouring of the Holy Spirit. A couple in church lied to the Holy Spirit and when their sin was revealed they immediately fell dead. It was unheard of. Peter got up to preach and three thousand souls were added to the church. Then a man who was unable to walk from his mother's womb was placed at the entry of the church, begging those who were entering and leaving for something to help his existence.

Peter and John didn't have silver or gold, instead they had something more powerful; the name of Jesus. The man expected to receive something from them and he got it. Peter commanded him to walk in the name of Jesus Christ and he grabbed him by his right hand and raised him up. "Immediately his feet and ankles were strengthened. With a leap, he stood upright and walked. He entered the church walking, leaping, and praising the Lord.

Special/Unusual Miracles

God worked special miracles by the hands of Paul. Handkerchiefs or aprons put on his body were given to people in need and the diseases and evil spirits went out of them. Then there was Peter's shadow. Sick people on beds and couches were laid in the street so Peter's shadow would overshadow them as he passed by. A multitude of sick and possessed people from cities outside Jerusalem came and everyone was healed (Acts 5:16). Notice everyone was healed.

It is unusual to hit a man with your fist in the stomach and he is healed. History has said this about Smith Wigglesworth. Many miracles of healings were done through this man's hands. There is no shortage of miracles once there is no shortage of believers that believe in the God of miracles. If there is a shortage of miracles, then believers need to start to believe and people need to be transferred from the kingdom of darkness to the kingdom of Christ. There are many biographical history books of men and women of faith in God who have given themselves totally over to God that the only thing left in them is the power of God. Will you be one of those?

There is David Hogan whose ministry has raised over five hundred people from the dead and still counting. He loves doing the impossible with God. People have been instantly healed of diseases and sicknesses unimaginable to many and some not known to man. The first time he ministered at our church there was a breakout of joy and laughter, and this was not conjured up nor created by any person. It was God. It was the first time I had such an experience. In that breakout of the Spirit there was healing and refreshing. David Hogan also lays his hands on handkerchiefs and the power of God lays resident in the handkerchiefs waiting to be ministered to people. When the handkerchief is placed on them, they are healed and delivered from demonic power.

There are numerous other people including bodies of believers that live in the hunger zone for miracles, healings, and deliverance. That's the place where God shows up. I remember one Sunday evening service at our church, the Spirit of God was moving. There was one particular place in the church where His presence was strongly felt. If you stood in that area you were healed of whatever disease you had. One time we had an elderly man that died in the service while I was ministering the word. A couple of people took him to the back of the church in our little bookstore. While I continued ministering the word, a couple of people raised him from the dead. Many people have been healed in our ministry. This is a very brief synopsis of what the Lord has done and is doing.

CHAPTER 17

Anyone Can Be Healed of Any Disease

Anyone can be healed of any disease. The Bible makes it very clear. If you understand your relationship with God; you'll always have victory. There will be tests of your faith; but the victory is always yours because it has already been won for you.

In the Old Covenant, every need of the children of Israel was met by God. God meeting their needs was a revelation of different aspects which was revealed by different names. In Genesis 22:13–14, God provided a sacrifice for Abraham. Abraham knew Him as the Lord will provide.

Judges 6:24, Jehovah Shalom which means Jehovah is peace.

Psalm 23:1, The Lord is my shepherd. Shepherd in Hebrew is *Ra'ah* meaning to tend a flock. In other words, Jehovah takes care of His own.

Ezekiel 48:35 is the Lord is there (Jehovah Shammah). Jehovah is everywhere. You can't hide from Him or run from Him. Wherever you go, He is there. How comforting!

Then Exodus 17:8–15 the Lord is My Banner or Jehovah Nissi.

When God appeared to Abram in Genesis 17:1 to change his name to Abraham, He appeared to him as God Almighty (El Shaddai). He appeared to him as the God with all might and power, strength; great.

Exodus 15:26, the Israelites would know Him as the Lord, your healer.

Everything Israel needed in their journey to the promised land, He provided. He was the solution to their problems and needs. He told them in Exodus 15:26, "If you diligently heed the voice of the Lord your God and do what is right in His sight, give ear to His commandments and keep all His statutes, I will put none of the diseases on you which I have brought on the Egyptians. For I am the Lord who heals you." Their key to success was to hear and do. It's still the same today.

If you hear today and do, you will be healed. You will also have the tools for your healing if you need healing. The Bible says in the book of Luke the people came 'to hear and to be healed.' In other words, the hearing brought the healing. That's why it's important we pay attention to what we hear. Luke 8:18 the Passion Translation states, "So pay careful attention to your hearts as you hear my teaching, for to those who have open hearts, even more revelation will be given to them until it overflows. And for those who do not listen with open hearts, what little light they imagine to have will be taken away." In other words be hungry for the Word of God and you will have revelation. Revelation is the source of healing, deliverance, breakthrough. Everything you receive from God by faith happens because of revelation. The Holy Spirit is the Spirit of Revelation.

Throughout history, God continually revealed Himself as the healer. The children of Israel under a covenant based on the blood of bulls and goats knew God as their healer; how much more, the body of Christ who lives under a better covenant which was established on better promises by the blood of the Lamb of God (Hebrews 8:6). Every time they needed healing they sought Jehovah Rapha and He healed them.

There are two primary ways a person can receive healing. They can be healed by faith in God's Word or through an intermediary (i.e., the gifts of the Spirit, laying on of hands, prayer of faith, etc.). God has made a way for every person to be healed of every disease. He is "no respecter of persons" (Acts 10:34). Almighty God can change body parts, create, resurrect or repair body parts. There's no shortage of resurrection power in God. He is the resurrection and the life (John 11:25).

Healing is yours; miracles are yours. That is part of your inheritance. It's time to be healed so your life can be lived to its fullest.

CHAPTER 18

The Power of Prophecies: The Messiah's Entrance into the Earth

God prophesied the woman's seed would bruise the serpent's head. We know that in the curse redemption for man was also spoken. The serpent knew it as well. Throughout history, he has tried to remove anyone or any peoples who appeared to possibly be the fulfillment of the prophecy. Several times in history, satanic people and leaders have tried to destroy the Jews to no avail. No one can destroy who God has blessed. Furthermore, through Abraham's seed, the world is blessed spiritually and naturally. Jesus is the fulfillment of prophecies that started in the garden of Eden and continued throughout generations until He manifested to the world in Matthew, Mark, Luke, and John.

The Word of God says, "But when the fullness of time was come, God sent forth his Son, made of a woman, made under the law, to redeem them that were under the law, that we might receive the adoption of sons." Everything was in its right place. The history that needed to happen had taken place. The political climate Jesus came into the earth was in its right place. Everything was in alignment for His coming; that's why He came when He did.

It's the same with every one of us. We are here in this earth at this time because everything was aligned for us at this present time to be here now. It was God's plan—His doing, because each of us has something to contribute to this earth that He created. None of us are accidents. God knew us before we were even in our mother's womb. He even has a book with our body parts in it (Psalm 139:15–16). It doesn't matter how you came into the earth. What matters is what you are going to do with what He placed within you to bless the earth.

Your body parts in His book are not sick. He doesn't make anything sick. It's not in His nature. "Every good gift and every perfect gift is from above and comes down from the Father of lights, with whom there is no variation or shadow of turning" (James 1:17, NKJV). He hasn't changed His mind about you. He wants you healthy, and He needs you healthy so you can fully manifest your contribution to earth, not live your life under the cloud of sickness or disease.

I have not written this book just to teach you and show you what God has said. I also wrote this book because I can empathize with people who were born into the earth sick and diseased, and just want to have a day or week feeling well. I cried that several times. If I could just have a day—a week is even better—where I can feel well. For me that meant not knowing I had a body—no pain, no discomfort, no machine to help me, no medication. All I wanted was to feel well.

Like God heard Ishmael, a teenager, when Abraham sent him away, God also heard my cry and responded. You're never too young or too old to cry out to God and start seeking Him for help. Never forget it's the desperate ones—those who are tired and had enough of a disease or sickness controlling their lives—who walk in their inheritance of healing, health, immunity.

CHAPTER 19

Limitless God, Limitless Children

If you are born of the spirit of God, you have His DNA. That means nothing is impossible to you. The word of God says, "Out of the heart flows the issues of life" (Proverbs 4:23). That's where the life of God is, and that is what you have to protect at all cost. Your heart is the place where the spirit of God resides. It's the place from where He speaks to you. It's the place where His healing power resides. That's why it must be protected. You protect it with your words because the enemy will try to pierce through it with words.

It's important that you don't allow anyone to speak words that will cause you to doubt God's word and His ability and desire for you to be healed and walk in divine health. Why would He not want you healed if He is the healer and His healing power resides in you? And He loves you so much that He sacrificed His best for you. Don't listen to religion that says, "It might not be God's will to heal you." If it might not be His will to heal you then He wouldn't be dwelling in you. Furthermore, why did Jesus go to the cross? Why does Isaiah 53:5 state, "By His stripes we are healed?" Then Peter states in 1 Peter 2:24, "Who His own self bare our sins in his own body on the tree, that we, being dead to sins, should live unto righteousness: by whose stripes you were healed."

Jesus healed everyone who came to Him for healing. He never told anyone, "No, not today." Matthew 8:16 says, "He cast out the spirits with His word and healed all that were sick." *All* means all.

THE TRUTH ABOUT YOUR HEALING

Once you truly believe you were healed, you will experience it in your body. In Mark 11:23–24, the key word that stands out is *believe*. And it's in reference to "believe before you see." This is the exact opposite of the natural man. But you are not natural. You are spiritual.

One morning in my time with the Lord, the spirit of the Lord said to me, "I have placed no restrictions on you. Whatever restrictions exists is because You put them there." I was shocked when He said it to me. I know the scriptures, but the way He said it impacted me, and those scriptures had new meaning to me. Jesus's death, burial, and resurrection made all impossibilities—possibilities. What is the natural man's impossibility is the spiritual man's possibility.

ABOUT THE AUTHOR

Adelle was born and raised on the island of St. Thomas, the US Virgin Islands. At the age of twelve, she made Jesus the Lord of her life. Her hunger and experiences with the Lord were very strong. Her first missionary trip was at the age of thirteen. That was where she learned about and saw the power of God in operation. Her appetite for the supernatural power and presence of God has not waned. She believes we are to have the same fellowship with God that Adam had, walking, and talking together. She currently resides between Arkansas and the island of St. Thomas in the US Virgin Islands and continues the work of the ministry. She's authored several books.

Books written by Adelle

The Good News for the Whole World
Now That You Are…
When the devil says No, God says 'Yes'
Surviving Your Seasons of Change
63 Days ± to Your Healing
Immunity

Adelle can be reached at adellebrown37@gmail.com